THE SANTORINI VOLCANO
AND THE DESOLATION OF
MINOAN CRETE

Dedicated to
SPYRIDON MARINATOS

THE SANTORINI VOLCANO AND THE DESOLATION OF MINOAN CRETE

by
D. L. PAGE
Regius Professor of Greek and Master of Jesus College Cambridge

THE SOCIETY FOR THE PROMOTION OF HELLENIC STUDIES
31–34 Gordon Square, London W.C.1
1970

© 1970 The Society for the Promotion of Hellenic Studies

Printed in Great Britain by
Alden & Mowbray Ltd
at The Alden Press, Oxford

Distributed by
International University Booksellers Ltd., 39 Store St., London W.C.1

CONTENTS

Foreword	vi
List of Illustrations and Acknowledgements	vii
I Crete: Destruction and Desolation	1
II Santorini: the Volcano	13
III Santorini: the Buried Town	24
IV Crete: How the End came	35
Bibliography	45

FOREWORD

The chapters of this book are the four Lord Northcliffe Lectures in Literature, delivered in University College London in February 1970. The Lectures were composed without any thought of publication (for I am an amateur in this field), and their form may be thought unsuitable; but I have not adapted them, except for the omission of a few jocose parentheses. I have reduced the number of illustrations by about a third.

Giving the Lord Northcliffe Lectures is a most enjoyable experience, and I am glad to have this opportunity of expressing my gratitude to all concerned, especially to the Provost and Professor Eric Handley for their genial and abundant hospitality. My warmest thanks are due also to Professor Eric Turner, and to the Hellenic Society of which he is President, for undertaking publication of the Lectures. To Dr Brian Sparkes, editor of the *Journal of Hellenic Studies*, I owe a more than ordinary obligation: as I was abroad for five months in the summer, Dr Sparkes took charge of the preparation of the book for the Press, and did everything much quicker and better than I should have done.

Accident deprived me of my own photographs in 1969: Dr Stubbings, Dr Redfrew and Mr Hammond most generously came to my rescue on the site, and many deficiencies could be supplied from among the incomparable photographs published by Mr Luce in *The End of Atlantis*.

I have frequently referred in the text to 'the Thera Congress'. In September 1969 I had the great good fortune to attend, in Greece, an international conference of scientists and archaeologists concerned with all aspects of the Santorini volcano. The Congress was organized and led by Professor Marinatos, who has most generously allowed me to make full use of his materials; I dedicate this book to him as a small token of gratitude for his friendship and for all that I have learnt from him.

LIST OF ILLUSTRATIONS AND ACKNOWLEDGEMENTS

Permission to reproduce illustrations was promptly and freely given by publishers and institutions, and we are grateful to them for their ready cooperation.

Of the private individuals to whom we are indebted for photographs, a special word of thanks is owed to J. V. Luce who at short notice loaned us the original transparencies for the cover and for pls. 6a, 6c, 7c, 7d, 8a, 10b, all of which had appeared in *The End of Atlantis*.

Text Figures

Fig. 1 Crete
2 Tylissos, plan of 'House A' (Sp. Marinatos, *Crete and Mycenae* [Thames and Hudson] p. 139, fig. 15)
3 Sklavókampo, plan (J.W. Graham, *The Palaces of Crete* [Princeton University Press] pl. 32; permission from Professor Graham)
4 Palaekastro, plan (*BSA* lx (1965) pl. 65; permission from the Trustees and M. Popham)
5 Destruction and abandonment of Minoan sites
6 Conventional time-table of Minoan periods
7 Revised time-table of Late Minoan I–II
8 Santorini: distribution of the tephra-layer
9 Santorini: stratification of the tephra-layer
10 Stages in the development of a caldera (F. M. Bullard, *Volcanoes in history, in theory, in eruption* [Nelson] p. 73, fig. 4; permission from University of Texas Press)
11 Cracatoa and the adjacent coasts (redrawn from R. Furneaux, *Krakatoa* [Secker and Warburg] plate following p. 128 = *The Royal Society Report* fig. 9; permission from the Royal Society)
12 Cracatoa: the area of the ash-deposit (F. M. Bullard, *op. cit.* p. 82, fig. 8)
13 Santorini: sites of the excavations
14 Excavations on the south coast of Therasia, by M. Fouqué in 1867 (F. Fouqué, *Santorin et ses éruptions* p. 96)
15 Excavations at Balos, by MM. Mamet and Gorceix (F. Fouqué, *op. cit.* p. 119)
16 Excavations in a ravine south of Acrotiri, by M. Fouqué and MM. Mamet and Gorceix (F. Fouqué, *op. cit.* p. 109)
17 Excavation in a ravine south of Acrotiri, by MM. Mamet and Gorceix (F. Fouqué, *op. cit.* p. 116)
18 Acrotiri: diagram of the excavation-area
19 Distribution of cores containing young layers of tephra (redrawn from *Submarine Geology and Physics: Proceedings of the Seventeenth Symposium of the Colston Research Society*, 'The Santorini Tephra' by D. Ninkovich and B. C. Heezen, fig. 163)

LIST OF ILLUSTRATIONS

Colour Illustrations

Cover   Santorini, the cliffs of pumice and ash in the quarries at Phira (J. V. Luce, *The End of Atlantis* [Thames and Hudson] pl. IV)

Plate A1   Zakro, the palace (S. Alexiou, N. Platon and H. Guanella, *Ancient Crete* [Thames and Hudson] p. 181)

Plate A2   Zakro, rock-crystal ritual vessel (Alexiou, Platon and Guanella, *op. cit.* p. 187)
- B1   Zakro, stone vase with wild goat (Alexiou, Platon and Guanella, *op. cit.* p. 193)
- B2   Zakro, bull's head of black chlorite (Alexiou, Platon and Guanella, *op. cit.* p. 180)
- C1   Santorini, from Phira to Therasia
- C2   Santorini, the northern tip of the crescent
- D1   Santorini, looking north from Phira
- D2   Santorini, the crater face and houses on the rim

Black and White Illustrations

Plate 1a   Staircase in 'House C', Tylissos (J. Hazzidakis, *Les villas minoennes de Tylissos* [Paris 1934] pl. IX)
- 1b   Nirou Khani (Sp. Marinatos, *Crete and Mycenae* [Thames and Hudson] pl. 65)
- 1c   Villa of the lily-frescoes, Amnisos (Marinatos, *op. cit.* pl. 64)
- 1d   Lily-fresco, Amnisos (Marinatos, *op. cit.* pl. XXII)
- 2a   Displaced and distorted foundations, Amnisos (*Praktika* 1932, p. 92, fig. 10)
- 2b   Gournia (S. Alexiou, N. Platon and H. Guanella, *Ancient Crete* [Thames and Hudson] p. 152)
- 2c   Terracotta figurine, Gournia (Alexiou, Platon and Guanella, *op. cit.* p. 203)
- 2d   Pseira, the island (Alexiou, Platon and Guanella, *op. cit.* p. 157)
- 3a   Pseira, the town (R. B. Seager, *Excavations in the island of Pseira, Crete* pl. IV)
- 3b   Mochlos (Alexiou, Platon and Guanella, *op. cit.* p. 35)
- 3c   Phaestos (Marinatos, *op. cit.* pl. XVIII)
- 3d   Mallia (Marinatos, *op. cit.* pl. 58)
- 4a   Patterns on LM Ia pottery (A. D. Lacy, *Greek Pottery in the Bronze Age* [Methuen] fig. 45; permission from Mrs Pendlebury)
- 4b   Patterns on LM Ib pottery (Lacy, *op. cit.* fig. 46; permission from Mrs Pendlebury)
- 4c   LM II 'Palace Style' jar, from Knossos (Lacy, *op. cit.* fig. 48b; permission from Society of Antiquaries of London)
- 4d   LM I Octopus-flask, from Palaekastro (Marinatos, *op. cit.* pl. 87)
- 5a   Santorini, from the air (J. V. Luce, *The End of Atlantis* [Thames and Hudson] pl. 16, from an air photograph by H. E. Edgerton)
- 5b   Santorini, the summit of the active volcano
- 5c   Santorini, the eruption of 1926
- 5d   Santorini, the way up the cliff at Phira
- 6a   Santorini, the face of the ash-layer (Luce, *op. cit.* pl. II)
- 6b   Santorini, the face of the ash-layer (L. Knidlberger, *Santorin* [Schloendorn Verlags-G.m.b.H.] opposite p. 157)
- 6c   Santorini, erosion on the surface of the pumice-layer (Luce, *op. cit.* pl. 19)
- 7a   Bronze blade with gold inlay, from Santorini (Luce, *op. cit.* pl. 43)
- 7b   Acrotiri, the ravine from the south (photograph by N. Hammond)
- 7c   Acrotiri, the cliffs of pumice and ash (Luce, *op. cit.* pl. 50)
- 7d   Acrotiri, the bed of the ravine (Luce, *op. cit.* pl. 52)

LIST OF ILLUSTRATIONS

8a   Acrotiri, the angle of a house-wall (Luce, *op. cit.* pl. VIII)
8b   Acrotiri, two walls (photograph by C. Renfrew)
8c   Acrotiri, two walls (photograph by C. Renfrew)
8d   Acrotiri, west–east wall (photograph by F. H. Stubbings)
9a   Acrotiri, monkey, wall-painting (Sp. Marinatos, *Excavations at Thera: second preliminary report* pl. B 1)
9b   Acrotiri, flying bird, wall-painting (Marinatos, *op. cit.* pl. B 2)
9c   Acrotiri, man and palm tree, wall-painting (Marinatos, *op. cit.* pl. B 3)
9d   Acrotiri, a flagstoned floor (*Athens Annals of Archaeology* 1968.3 Frontispiece, upper picture)
10a   Acrotiri, basement with window at street level (photograph by F. H. Stubbings)
10b   Acrotiri, interior service-stair (Luce, *op. cit.* pl. VII)
11a   Acrotiri, decorated strainer (Marinatos, *op. cit.* pl. E 8)
11b   Acrotiri, kymbe with swallows (Marinatos, *op. cit.* pl. C 8 and 17.2)
11c   Acrotiri, polychrome jug (Marinatos, *op. cit.* pl. A)
11d   Acrotiri, kymbe with dolphins (Marinatos, *op. cit.* pl. C 7 and 11.2)
12a   Acrotiri, spherical jug (Marinatos, *op. cit.* pl. D 1)
12b   Acrotiri, spherical jug (Marinatos, *op. cit.* pl. D 4)
12c   Acrotiri, spherical jug (Marinatos, *op. cit.* pl. D 5)
12d   Acrotiri, goblets and a cup (Marinatos, *op. cit.* pl. D 7)
13a   Acrotiri, pot with pierced base (Marinatos, *op. cit.* pl. E 2 and 10.1)
13b   Acrotiri, jug with pendent sprays (Marinatos, *op. cit.* pl. E 4)
13c   Acrotiri, jug with reed-like plants (Marinatos, *op. cit.* pl. E 5)
13d   Acrotiri, sherds with 'Linear A' script (Marinatos, *op. cit.* pl. 38.1)
14a   Acrotiri, doorway in wall affected by earthquake (photograph by C. Renfrew)
14b   Acrotiri, collapsed rubble wall (photograph by F. H. Stubbings)
14c   Acrotiri, displaced wall-blocks (photograph by N. Hammond)
14d   Acrotiri, collapsed building (photograph by N. Hammond)
15a   Acrotiri, window used as entrance (photograph by N. Hammond)
15b   Acrotiri, blocked staircase (photograph by N. Hammond)
15c   Acrotiri, 'Street of the Telchines' (photograph by Sp. Marinatos)
15d   Acrotiri, 'Street of the Telchines', cleared (photograph by F. H. Stubbings)
16a   Acrotiri, room occupied by 'squatters' (photograph by C. Renfrew)
16b   Acrotiri, a row of jars (photograph by C. Renfrew)
16c   Acrotiri, jars cracked by the heat (Sp. Marinatos, *Excavations at Thera: first preliminary report* fig. 25)
16d   Acrotiri, broken vessels (Sp. Marinatos, *Excavations at Thera: second preliminary report* pl. 15.2)
17a   Acrotiri, lion's head vessel *in situ* (Marinatos, *op. cit.* fig. 10)
17b   Acrotiri, lion's head vessel (Marinatos, *op. cit.* pl. 37.1)
17c   Acrotiri, large decorated container (Marinatos, *op. cit.* pl. 25.1)
17d   Acrotiri, small figurine in bottom of container (Marinatos, *op. cit.* pl. 24.2)
18a   Acrotiri, circular table with depressions (Marinatos, *op. cit.* pl. 31.1)
18b   Acrotiri, nippled jug (Marinatos, *op. cit.* pl. 36.1)
18c   Acrotiri, libation jug (Marinatos, *op. cit.* pl. 31.2)
18d   Acrotiri, conical rhyton (Marinatos, *op. cit.* pl. E 6)
19   Acrotiri, window and door in Western Tunnel (Marinatos, *op. cit.* pl. 32)
20   Cloud from the cone of Bezymianny, 1956 (K. Wilcoxson, *Volcanoes* [Cassell] plate following p. 160)

I Crete: Destruction and Desolation

If you go to the island of Santorini, about sixty-five miles north of Crete, you see plain evidence of one of the biggest volcanic eruptions on earth since the last ice-age. If you go to Crete, you find that almost every place in its eastern half which was inhabited in a certain period was destroyed in that period. The suggestion that these two phenomena are related as cause and effect—that Minoan Crete was destroyed by the action of the volcano at Santorini—was first made by Professor Marinatos in the nineteen-thirties. For a long time few people took much notice; but in recent years the topic has become fashionable, and the causal connexion is now widely accepted. I believe that much work remains to be done before a final answer can be given; in the meantime I limit myself to the assembly of basic facts on which a conclusion must be based.

First, I consider a question which is not to be taken for proved—the basic question, whether there ever was a period of more or less total destruction in Crete in the fifteenth century B.C. I visit some of the devastated places, and about each of them I ask three questions: first, when was it destroyed? Secondly, what was the cause of its destruction? And thirdly—a specially important question—was it finally, or for some time, abandoned? There might be a variety of possible reasons for the destruction of numerous places in a short time; if destruction was followed by abandonment, the range of possible causes is reduced. If we are satisfied that the greater part of Minoan Crete was not only destroyed within a short period of time but also abandoned at least for some years, the inquiry can proceed.

Fig. 1

Now, in order to judge what effect a volcano might have, it is necessary to ascertain what sort of volcano it is. So in the second lecture I go to Santorini and study the volcano at close quarters. It is a fascinating place, and very helpful.

Since 1967 excavations conducted by Professor Marinatos have unearthed a prosperous settlement in Santorini, buried under pumice and ash. In the third lecture I visit

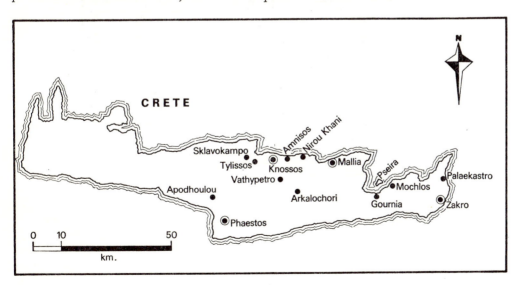

Fig. 1 Crete

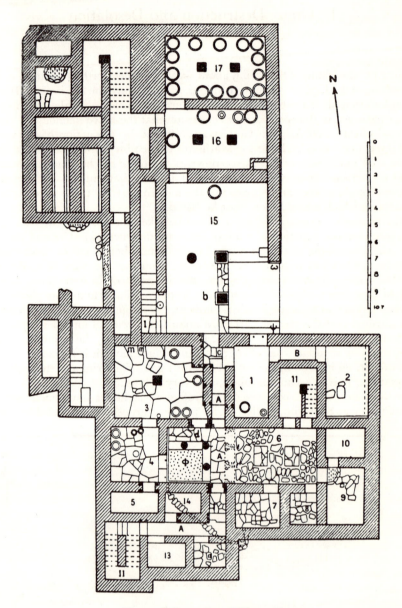

Fig. 2 Tylissos, plan of 'House A'

I CRETE: DESTRUCTION AND DESOLATION

these excavations and ask whether they have anything relevant to say; they have, and thereby make our task the harder.

By this time I shall have established (or not) that a large part of Minoan Crete was destroyed in a certain period and abandoned for some time thereafter, and that the volcano at Santorini could have been the cause. It will then be rational to consider, in the last lecture, the final question,—not only could the volcano have destroyed Crete, but did it, and (if so) how, and what exactly is the evidence for this conclusion?

Accordingly I begin with a tour of some of the devastated sites in Minoan Crete.

1   *Tylissos*[1]

About seven miles west of Heraclion is the site of Tylissos. Here, very close together, are the remains of three grand houses. 'House A' was furnished with entrance-hall (ψ-ω); hall (15) with stone staircase leading to an upper floor where the family lived (the servants occupied the ground-floor); main corridor (A) leading to a living-room (6), store-rooms (3-5), light-well (φ), other rooms, one of them containing bronze baths, the biggest ever found. Drainage passes from room to room in stone conduits. The whole structure is very costly. It covers about two thousand square feet. The exterior walls average $2\frac{1}{2}$ feet in thickness of stone. The solidity of the building is well illustrated by a picture of an interior staircase in 'House C'.

Fig. 2

Plate 1a

This was a mansion designed to serve a rich man's family for ever and a day; yet it collapsed not very long after it was built. When was it destroyed? In the period called 'Late Minoan I b'. What destroyed it? A violent conflagration; signs of it are visible to this day. Was it ever re-occupied? The site was abandoned for some time; it was then re-settled by a people whose architecture and pottery are different from the past. What happened at Tylissos in Late Minoan I b? Later on we shall have to define what we mean by this term; according to the conventional time-table it covers the period from 1500 to 1450 B.C.

2   *Sklavókampo*[2]

The present road from Tylissos to Anógeia was being constructed in 1930. About six miles west of Tylissos the road-makers dug past, and partly through, a large Minoan mansion in a valley between foot-hills of Mount Ida. The place, almost uninhabited, is called Sklavókampo. The road-works ruined much of the mansion; the rest is said to have been 'ruthlessly destroyed' in the second World War. There is not much to be seen today.

Fig. 3

It is an interesting house. The construction was not worthy of the architect's plan, which was original and pleasing. He deserved a richer or a more ambitious client. The exterior walls are crudely built of stone; inside, there are no wall-paintings and no paved floors; staircases are wooden, not of stone. Still, it is a big and solid house, in two storeys. The north wall is four feet thick. The illustration shows the main entrance (1), main living-room (4), room for religious ritual (8); staircase, and lavatory beneath it; store-rooms (11-12); veranda with a fine view to the north (13). There seems to be no door (though there may have been a service-hatch) to the servants' quarters, of which the most interesting feature is the *compluvium*, a largely-roofed light-well (15).

The surviving contents of the house are not abundant. Most remarkable are certain clay sealings, nearly forty of them, some very beautiful; these sealings relate the mansion very closely to other places on our list,—Zakro, Gournia, Hagia Triadha.

When was this mansion destroyed? In Late Minoan I b, perhaps fifty years after it was built. What destroyed it? An exceptionally violent conflagration; nowhere, except at

---

[1]Hazzidakis, *Les villas minoennes de Tylissos* (Paris 1934); *Tylissos à l'époque minoenne* (Paris 1921); 'Αρχ. 'Εφ. 1912, 197-233; Kirsten, *RE* vii A 1713 ff.; Robinson, *RE* suppl. vii 239; Pendlebury 228; Graham 60 f.; Marinatos[1] 140.

[2]Marinatos, 'Αρχ. 'Εφ. 1939-47, 69-96; Graham 70 f.; Robinson, *RE* suppl. vii 239.

I CRETE: DESTRUCTION AND DESOLATION

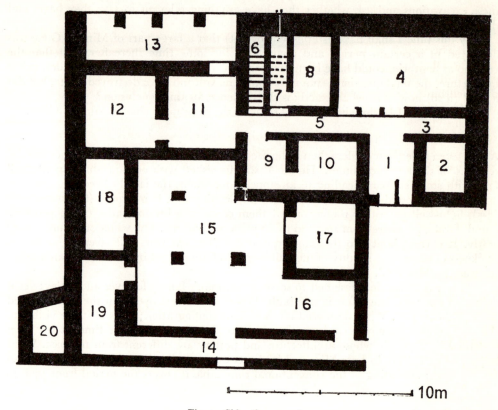

Fig. 3   Sklavókampo, plan

Gournia, is the evidence for this more impressive. Was it ever re-built and re-occupied? It was abandoned there and then for ever.

3 *Nirou Khani*[3]

Nirou Khani lies on the coast road about eight miles east of Heraclion. Here are the remains of a grand mansion; forty rooms on the ground floor, covering more than three thousand square feet. The stone walls were lined with gypsum and elaborately painted. Floors were flagstoned. Stone stairs led to an upper storey. This was one of the most luxuriously constructed buildings in Minoan Crete, except only the great palaces. It is in one other respect exceptional and enigmatic. In one room were found four bronze axes, the biggest so far known. These are ritual objects, and so are the contents of another room—between forty and fifty tripod-tables for holy offerings neatly stacked against the wall. We are not now asking why the mansion was stocked with these and other ritual objects, far too numerous for personal use. Our questions at present are, first, when was this mansion destroyed? In Late Minoan I b. What destroyed it? There was a violent fire.[4] Was it ever re-occupied? It was abandoned for ever; and whoever abandoned it left many objects of much piety and some of great value on the floors. What happened at Nirou Khani in Late Minoan I b?

Plate 1b

[3]Xanthudides, Ἀρχ. Ἐφ. 1922, 1-25; *AA* 1922, 323 ff.; Evans *PM* i 437, ii 279 ff.; Hutchinson 284; Graham 58 f.; Pendlebury 190, 228, 237; Marinatos¹ 66; Robinson, *RE* suppl. vii 239.
[4]Xanthudides, Ἀρχ. ’φ. Ε1922, 9.

I CRETE: DESTRUCTION AND DESOLATION

4   *Amnisos*[5]

Returning to Heraclion by the coast road we pause at Amnisos, three miles west of Nirou Khani. This was an important harbour in Minoan days; long looked-for by archaeologists, first unearthed by the snout of a providential pig in 1932. Among its buildings, concentrate on the villa with the lily-frescoes. These are the ruins of an elegant house, neat in design and well built. Delicate paintings covered the walls of the principal room. A flagstoned veranda overlooked the sea. A stone staircase led to an upper floor.   *Plate 1c*
   Plate 1d

This villa was built in the last phase of the Middle Minoan period. Its outer walls rest on large blocks of limestone, six feet long and three feet square. It was built to last; but it came to a premature and violent end. The walls bulged, and the house collapsed. Stone bases for wooden columns are blackened by fire. Of the big foundation-blocks, some are oddly twisted out of line, others are wholly dislodged.   *Plate 2a*

The date of destruction is Late Minoan I, but whether the earlier phase, I a, or the later, I b, is not absolutely decided. The cause of destruction was fire, certainly, in part; the dislodging of the big foundation-blocks might be caused either by earthquake or by flood-waves of exceptional violence. The villa was never re-built or re-occupied.

5   *Gournia*[6]

On a low hill-top close to the sea, looking north over the beautiful bay of Mirabello, is the Minoan town of Gournia; not a palace or a mansion but the whole of a little village (it is less than two hundred yards long), uncovered by three American ladies in the earliest days of Cretan excavation, 1901-4. The site was continuously occupied from the earliest Minoan period onwards. It flourished particularly in the last phase of the Middle Minoan period; and in Late Minoan I it was much as you see it today, except (as so often elsewhere) that the houses are not preserved above the first storey. There was one very grand house, the residence of a person in authority. The rest are small and tightly packed together; they are the houses and workshops of carpenters, coppersmiths, weavers, masons, potters, farmers and fishermen. Of all sites in Crete this is the most homely and haunted, the one most recently vacated (you might think) by the last Minoan ghost.   *Plate 2b*

This busy noisy little town came to a sudden end. Carpenters and coppersmiths abandoned their workshops, actually leaving their precious tools on the floor. A thousand years of life and labour at Gournia ended wholly and abruptly—when? In Late Minoan I b. What destroyed it? There was a fire of quite exceptional violence.[7] Was it ever re-occupied? After an appreciable interval men returned to the site, but in small numbers. There are a few houses of Late Minoan III; one of them is very grand. They stayed a short time; then the site was abandoned for ever.[8] The futile gods were left standing on their little shelf in the prayer-house. The illustration shows one of them, a female;[9] bewildered,   *Plate 2c*
you may think, and conscious of failure. We do not take her with us when we leave. We have no more use for her. We must find a new home elsewhere, and we shall need new gods. This one can be left to gaze for ever on the desolation from which it was her plain duty to protect us.

[5]Marinatos, *PAE* 1932, 76-94; *AA* 1933, 290; *BCH* lvii (1933) 292-5; Hutchinson 274 f.; Graham 68 f.
[6]*Gournia, Vasiliki, and other prehistoric sites on the isthmus of Hierapetra, Crete: Excavations of the Wells-Houston-Cramp expeditions*, 1901, 1903, 1904, by Harriet Boyd Hawes, Blanche E. Williams, Richard B. Seager, Edith H. Hall; published by the American Exploration Society, Free Museum of Science and Art (Philadelphia 1908); Graham 47 ff.; Hutchinson 190.
[7]*Gournia* 21; see p. 38 below.
[8]Desborough 169: 'The re-occupation period of Gournia ... belongs rather to L.M. III a, and is not very extensive. Even less so are the traces of L.M. III b habitation ... and they cannot be shown to continue into L.M. III c'.
[9] Some call her a 'votary' rather than a goddess.

I CRETE: DESTRUCTION AND DESOLATION

6 *Pseira*[10]

Plate 2d

Plate 3a

The island called Pseira, waterless[11] and barren today, lies in the bay of Mirabello about two miles north of Gournia. Here is one of the best-preserved of Minoan sites. If it were easier of access it would be one of the most frequented and admired. At Pseira as at Gournia almost the whole of a little town was unearthed. A stairway leads up from the tiny harbour to the crest of a rocky point. Houses cluster thickly along the steep sides of the promontory and its spine. No great mansion was found, let alone a palace. This was a village mainly of craftsmen and sea-traders. Its history begins in the Early Minoan period; when does it end? Pseira flourished greatly in Late Minoan I b, and in that same period its history ends. Destruction was sudden and total. There is no clear evidence of the cause. The island was abandoned in Late Minoan I b; it has not been re-occupied from that day to this.[12]

7 *Mochlos*[13]

Plate 3b

The small island of Mochlos, perhaps joined to the mainland in Minoan times, is now divided from it by about 150 yards of shallow water. Here was a small town, with many tombs of various ages which yielded a rich harvest of treasures, especially of work in gold and stone. Mochlos may claim to have produced, in the Early Minoan periods, some of the most skilful makers of stone vases the world has ever seen. The history of the place is otherwise wholly obscure, but there is no doubt about its history's end: Mochlos prospered for a thousand years, and suddenly it prospered no more. The end came in Late Minoan I b. The cause of destruction is not known. There is no evidence that anyone ever lived there again until the Roman occupation of Crete.[14]

8 *Palaekastro*[15]

Fig. 4

On a coastal plain in the far east of Crete lie the remains of a relatively large Minoan town of small houses and narrow, sometimes winding, streets. This is another very old settlement; it was indeed continuously occupied from the Early Minoan periods—till when? Till Late Minoan I b. That is, in the words of the town's latest excavators 'the great destruction-period'.[16] The cause of destruction is most plainly visible in the building-complex called 'Block N': in the inner hall there are 'stones . . . calcined by the very intense fire which destroyed the house, and over the floors was a layer of black ash';[17] compartment no. 9 in this block had an 'exceptionally thick and heavy layer of black ash';[18] similar tokens of a violent conflagration were to be seen elsewhere in the block and in the rest of the town. The devastated site was sparsely re-occupied in the following period, Late Minoan III a; the neighbouring acropolis of Kastri perhaps less sparsely.[19]

9 *Phaestos*[20]

I conclude this survey with brief notes on the great palaces. First, Phaestos, a monumental building on a steep acropolis looking north to the range of Mount Ida and east over the

---

[10]R. B. Seager, *Excavations in the Island of Pseira, Crete* (Philadelphia 1910); Hutchinson 154 f.

[11]Seager supposed that the Minoans 'were supplied by springs which have ceased to flow'. Slopes behind the town were certainly cultivated by the Minoans.

[12]There are remains of a Roman military camp still visible on the topmost ridge of the island and a small group (20 x 30 m.) of Roman buildings in the Minoan town. There is no evidence of occupation in the intervening period (Classical sherds on the S. and E. slopes, but no buildings; Pendlebury 354).

[13]R. B. Seager, *Explorations in the island of Mochlos* (Boston & New York 1912); Hutchinson 154 f.

[14]Pendlebury 365, 375.

[15]R. C. Bosanquet, *BSA* viii-xi (1901-5); *Suppl. Paper* i (1923); Sackett, Popham and Warren, *BSA* lx (1965) 248 ff.; Graham 69 f.; Hutchinson 146.

[16]*BSA* lx (1965) 249.   [17]*Ibid.* 265.   [18]*Ibid.* 260.

[19]Re-occupation of Kastri lasted into L.M. III c (Desborough 279; *BSA* lx [1965]).

[20]Pernier, *Il Palazzo Minoico di Festós* i (1935), II (1951); Levi, 'Gli Scavi a Festós negli anni 1958-60', *ASAA* from xxxix-xl, n.s. xxiii-xxiv (1961-62); Graham 34 ff.; Hutchinson 190 ff.; recent literature on Hagia Triadha, Cameron, *Kadmos* iv (1965) 8 nn. 5-8.

Plate 1a   Staircase in 'House C', Tylissos

Plate 1b   Nirou Khani

Plate 1c   Villa of the lily-frescoes, Amnisos

Plate 1d   Lily-fresco, Amnisos

Plate 2a Displaced and distorted foundations, Amnisos

Plate 2b Gournia

Plate 2c Terracotta figurine, Gournia

Plate 2d Pseira, the island

I CRETE: DESTRUCTION AND DESOLATION

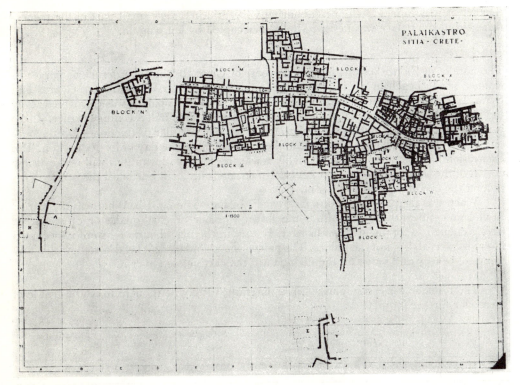

Fig. 4 Palaekastro, plan

whole of the plain of Mesara. Two miles to the west is a smaller palace called Hagia Triadha. We see both palaces in ruins; when were they destroyed? In the same period as all the other places. What was the cause? There is much evidence of burning, both at Phaestos and at Hagia Triadha.[21] Were they ever re-occupied? The surroundings of Phaestos were inhabited again fairly soon, but the palace was never re-built or re-occupied as a palace. Hagia Triadha was re-constructed before long and had a few more generations of prosperity.

Plate 3c

10 *Mallia*[22]

Close to the shore about twenty miles east of Heraclion lie the ruins of the palace called after the neighbouring village 'Mallia'; about the size of Phaestos, much smaller than Knossos and less luxuriously appointed, but still a massive and elaborate construction, with an adjacent town and burial-place and harbour. The staircases and stone-work are particularly fine.

Plate 3d

The ruins represent a building mainly of the Middle Minoan period. About the end of that period the palace was re-constructed, durable for hundreds of years beyond the time of its collapse. It was reduced to ruins in Late Minoan I b. The cause of destruction is not clear, except in so far as burning played a part in it.[23] Men returned and made

---

[21] Banti 567, *al.*

[22] Chapoutier and others, *Fouilles exécutées à Mallia* 1922-4 onwards (Paris 1928-); Graham 63 ff.; Hutchinson 184 ff.

[23] *Mallia 1922-4* 45, 'incendie' is given as the cause of destruction in L.M.I.; the date is more narrowly defined as L.M. I b in *Mallia 1925-6* 50 and in subsequent volumes.

B   7

I CRETE: DESTRUCTION AND DESOLATION

themselves new homes in the neighbouring villas and in a very small part of the palace-ruins;[24] but the palace was never re-built or occupied by kings again.

11 *Zakro*[25]

Plate A1

Plates A2, B1-2

The hamlet of Zakro lies on the eastern coast of Crete. Behind it, a ferocious gorge; in front, a sandy beach in a wide bay whose nearest neighbours eastward are Cyprus and Syria. In this remote and beautiful place, in 1961, a Minoan palace was discovered; only the fifth of its kind, and the first such discovery since Mallia half a century earlier. Zakro is much like the other palaces in design, but it has one peculiar distinction—it is the only one of the Cretan palaces which has not been looted since the day of its destruction. The excavation has therefore been most richly rewarding; a few illustrations will convey some notion of the skill and taste of Cretan craftsmen, not only here but in all the other places too, on the eve of the crack of doom.

When was the palace of Zakro destroyed? In Late Minoan I b. What was the cause? A violent conflagration, but also some force, whether of earthquake or of sea-flood, strong enough to topple great walls over. Houses in the neighbourhood were re-occupied after an interval, but not the palace. The palace was abandoned; it lay deserted, with many things of beauty and value on the floors, until the earth closed over it.

Fig. 5

The result so far is summarized in a diagram; it may be thought to establish at least a case for further inquiry.

Site	Tylissos	Nirou Khani	Sklavó-kampo	Amnisos, house of frescoes	Gournia	Pseira	Mochlos	Palae-kastro	Phaestos	Mallia	Zakro
Period of destruction in Late Minoan	I b	I b	I b	I a/b	I b	I b	I b	I b	I b	I b	I b
Cause of destruction	Fire	Fire	Fire	Quake or flood and fire	Fire	?	?	Fire	Quake and fire	Some evidence of burning	Quake or flood and fire
Abandoned, whether temporarily or permanent	temp.	perm.	perm.	perm.	temp.	perm.	perm.	temp.	perm.†	perm.†	perm.†

†—never re-built or re-occupied as Palaces.

Fig. 5 Destruction and abandonment of Minoan sites

I have left the Palace of Knossos to the end of this tour of Cretan sites. There is something problematic in its relation to the picture which seems to be taking shape. All the other places which I have mentioned (and some which I have not) were destroyed in Late Minoan I b, and it would be natural to suppose that Knossos was involved in the general ruin. But if, as many believe, the general ruin is to be dated somewhere near the middle of the fifteenth century B.C., it is certain that the sufferings of Knossos were relatively slight at that time. The palace and its neighbourhood were indeed damaged in Late Minoan I b, but the damage to the palace was soon repaired, and life at Knossos remained prosperous and colourful for two or three more generations. Not until Late Minoan III a (say, 1380 B.C.) was the palace of Knossos finally destroyed, never again to be the residence of kings.

It is not easy to understand how Knossos should be immune from serious injury while the palaces of Phaestos, Mallia, and Zakro, and great mansions in the neighbourhood of Knossos itself, were collapsing in sudden and—for most of them—final ruin. There is a problem here, too large for discussion within my present limits. I shall state very briefly what the problem is; and this is best done in the light of what I must anyway do next, which

---

[24]Desborough 169.
[25]N. Platon, *PAE* from 1961; Platon[1] *passim*; Platon[2] 163-7; Platon, Ἡ τελική καταστροφή τῶν Μινωικῶν ἀνακτόρων (Chania Congress 1967) i 220-8.

8

I CRETE: DESTRUCTION AND DESOLATION

is to define what I mean by the term 'Late Minoan I b'. For there are two questions still to be considered before the assembly of basic facts about the destruction of these Cretan places is complete. 'Late Minoan I b' covers a long period of time. To say that all these places were destroyed in Late Minoan I b is to say merely that they were destroyed within half a century according to the conventional time-table; and the time-range is really about double that. So our two questions are: what is the justification for saying that these places were all destroyed more or less simultaneously; and whereabouts within this long period is the point of simultaneous destruction (if there was one) to be placed?

	EARLY MINOAN		MIDDLE MINOAN		LATE MINOAN
I	2500–2400 B.C.	I	1950–1850 B.C.	I a	1550–1500 B.C.
II	2400–2100	II	1850–1750	I b	1500–1450
III	2100–1950	III	1750–1550	II	1450–1400
				III	1400–

Fig. 6 Conventional time-table of Minoan periods

The conventional time-table shows three periods with sub-divisions. These correspond to changes and developments in various arts and artefacts. The sequence of periods and sub-divisions is established objectively to a large extent by the strata in the earth from which things are taken, subjectively by judgements about technical and artistic developments. The mass of evidence is great; and although the periods could with advantage be differently named and divided,[26] there is no doubt that the sequence is true to life in broad outline and to a great extent in detail too. Nevertheless there remain some problems not yet wholly solved either by stratification or by aesthetics, and one of these problems confronts us when we try to say what we mean by the term 'Late Minoan I b' in the present context.

Fig. 6

The impression immediately given by the conventional time-table, that there were, within the period 1550 to 1400 B.C., three distinct phases of culture, each lasting fifty years, is misleading. Both the period-column and the date-column are over-simplified. The evidence on which the scheme is based is primarily ceramic—the shapes, techniques and decoration of pottery. The topic is complex, and the number of persons qualified to speak with authority is not large. I am not one of them. I mention only, and very briefly, those aspects of the decoration of painted pottery to which the experts themselves assign a leading part in debates about chronology.

In the first sub-division of the Late Minoan period, I a, decoration consists for the most part of linear designs—straight lines and wavy lines, spirals, circles, rosettes—or of floral designs—flowers, leaves, branches, grasses; or of combinations of the two types. The time-table obscures the fact that decoration of these types, linear and floral, remains common in most places throughout the whole period down to and beyond the beginning of Late Minoan III.

Plate 4a

In the next sub-division, I b, a decorative theme which had been relatively rare in the past becomes for a time very fashionable—the painting of sea-scapes with fishes, octopuses, sea-weed, rocks, shells. This, the Marine Style, is not common and apparently not of long duration. Not a single example of it had been found among the many thousands of pots from Knossos until Mr Hood in 1961 found a stratum of Marine Style in the Royal Road;[27] and this was mixed with pottery in the Floral Style. Marine Style represents not a break in development but merely an addition to the repertoire; and it forms a very small component of the total inventory.[28] There is nothing like enough to justify assigning to it

Plate 4b

---

[26] Platon's scheme has advantages: Neolithic 6000–2600 B.C.; pre-Palatial 2600–2000; First Palatial 2000–1700; Second Palatial 1700–1400; post-Palatial 1400–1150; sub-Minoan 1150–1000; all but the first and last with three sub-divisions each.
[27] *Archaeological Reports for 1961–2* 25
[28] Banti 502.

I CRETE: DESTRUCTION AND DESOLATION

half a century of production.[29] The later history of this period, I b, has been partly clarified by Mr Coldstream[30] in a recent discussion of pottery from the island of Cythera, where a pure deposit of this period shows (for the first time) the development of distinctive fashions foreshadowing some of the changes which are characteristic of the following period, Late Minoan II.

Late Minoan II has certain distinctive features,[31] among which the so-called 'Palace Style' is one of the most notable. The term 'Palace Style' was first used by Sir Arthur Evans to distinguish certain large and luxurious jars closely associated with the last days of the Palace of Knossos. Their decoration is much less naturalistic; you may see a helmet apparently floating in a sea-scape, or a starfish basking in the company of an axe. It is described by Doro Levi as a 'pompous style, with a touch of the baroque'.[32] Observe (for example) the frivolous and frilly object that passes for an octopus with painters of the Palace Style; an etiolated and simpering degenerate. Contrast with him his ancestor in the Marine Style, a lusty extrovert, full of bounce and braggadocio.

Plate 4c
Plate 4d

It is difficult for the layman to find his way about in this period. Some say that the Palace Style 'has no cultural significance except in the neighbourhood of Knossos' and that 'elsewhere pottery of L.M. I b style, or in some places L.M. I a style, persists without much change'. According to others the Palace Style is more or less widespread in Crete; Seager identified it at Pseira and Mochlos, Carr Bosanquet at Palaekastro, Vermeule at Zakro, Levi at a large number of other sites.[33] The fashion seems not to have lasted long in Crete; certainly not so long as the half-century commonly assigned to the period 'Late Minoan II'. There is 'simply not enough ... Palace Style to account for fifty years of workshop output'.[34] The predominant styles at the end of the whole period, down to the beginning of Late Minoan III, are developments of the fashions of I a and I b.

Fig. 7

A truer picture may therefore be given by a different sort of diagram, one which portrays the whole period as a continuum, within which the Marine and Palace Styles are episodes—'ripples across the surface of a more leisurely artistic growth'.[35] We replace the horizontal lines of separation by vertical lines of concurrence, and we abandon the tidy division of the whole into three half-centuries. We still allow the Floral Style to flourish for a long time before the Marine Style becomes fashionable, and we agree that the Marine Style is appreciably older than the Palace Style. But we do not know—at least within a couple of decades on either side of any likely point—the exact time when any of these styles began to become fashionable. If we want to define 'Late Minoan I b' more closely in the present context, we have only one clue to guide us: the pottery from the destruction-levels of our Cretan sites indicates that the general devastation of Crete occurred at a time when all three styles—Floral, Marine, and Palace—were more or less concurrent. Marine Style is found on all our sites except perhaps Amnisos, and the influence of Palace Style is plain on at least a third of them. The presence of Marine and Palace Style may be more significant than their absence, for neither is common, and absence from a particular site may well be fortuitous.

So the point (if there is one) must be placed within the latter half of this long period; but whereabouts? There is fundamental disagreement about that. Of the leading archaeologists, some place the general destruction of Crete roughly in the middle of the fifteenth century B.C. and the fall of Knossos seventy or eighty years later. Others assert that no distinction can be drawn between the pottery in the destruction-levels of Knossos and that of the other places; these therefore maintain that the general destruction of Crete occurred at the time of the final destruction of the Palace of Knossos, that is to say about 1380 B.C.,

---

[29]Hutchinson 282; Vermeule, *GBA* 142.
[30]*BICS* xvi (1969) 150 ff.   [31]Lacy 109 ff.   [32]Levi 260.
[33]Seager, *Pseira* i 21, *Mochlos* 91; *BSA Suppl. Paper* i 121 (Palaekastro); Hazzidakis, *Les villes minoennes de Tylissos* 37; Hutchinson 291; Vermeule, *GBA* 146; Levi 260; Lacy 91, 98, 103, *al.*
[34]Vermeule, *GBA* 144.   [35]Vermeule, *GBA* 145.

I CRETE: DESTRUCTION AND DESOLATION

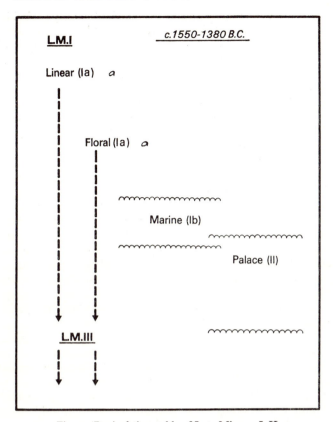

Fig. 7 Revised time-table of Late Minoan I–II

and there is then no need to suppose that Knossos escaped serious injury when all the other places were destroyed. I should like to believe this; but the trend of the most recent evidence and study is in the other direction, and it seems likely that the former opinion will prevail—that the general catastrophe occurred about the middle of the fifteenth century, and that Knossos, although its palace was damaged and although its neighbourhood must have been severely damaged, survived the catastrophe at that time and was quite soon restored to prosperity. This is the opinion which (after much study and still with some doubt) I have provisionally chosen to adopt. I conclude, therefore, that the general destruction of Crete occurred about 1450 B.C. I do not see how it is possible to be more precise; nor does it matter much. The more important question is whether there is any occasion for a precise date: are we really sure that all our Cretan sites were destroyed more or less simultaneously?

For an answer to this question we are dependent on the skill, experience, and judgement of experts in the arts and crafts of Minoan Crete. A variety of technical and aesthetic criteria, confirmed in part by stratification, enables the archaeologist to distinguish earlier from later and to associate like with like. Thus it may be said with confidence that the latest artefacts from Tylissos were made at about the same time as those from Nirou Khani; that the pottery in the destruction-levels at Pseira, Mochlos, Gournia and Palaekastro show the same styles and techniques in vogue at the same stage of development in all four places; and so forth.

Now while the results actually achieved may seem to the layman to fall short of proof that the disasters were more or less simultaneous on all our sites, they do narrow the time-

I CRETE: DESTRUCTION AND DESOLATION

limits. Indeed they narrow the limits so far as to make it obviously probable that the disasters occurred within a short space of time, and quite possible that they were simultaneous. Most of the leading archaeologists go much further than this, asserting in plain terms that all our sites (except, in the opinion of some, Knossos) were destroyed more or less simultaneously.[36] I am content to say merely that the evidence is strongly in favour of a short space of time. I do not think that it is (or could be) proved that the disasters were simultaneous; but I do think it proved that it is possible that they were. And from this it follows that it is a rational question to ask whether we know of any cause which could have devastated Crete in a short time—whether 'short time' means minutes, as in earthquake, or months, as perhaps during volcanic action, or a few years, as in war.

First, then, might all these Cretan places have been destroyed by the hand of man? Certainly not all of them were; Zakro, for example, which was left unlooted; nor were the big foundation-blocks at Amnisos dislodged by man. For the rest, you might entertain the notion of a war resulting in the destruction of every known place except Knossos; and you might then naturally suppose that Knossos conquered and destroyed the rest. If this were the true account, the destroyers were surely Mycenaean Greeks from the mainland ruling over Knossos; written tablets in the Greek language, contemporary with the last days of the Palace of Knossos about 1380 B.C., prove Mycenaean occupation of Knossos for some time past. Suppose that the Mycenaeans invaded Crete and occupied Knossos about the middle of the fifteenth century; are we to believe that they systematically destroyed all the other palaces, the towns in the far east of Crete, the great mansions and harbour-towns in the neighbourhood of Knossos itself? Doro Levi calls such a theory 'an absurdity needing no further discussion';[37] the best that can be said about it is that it is very improbable. The Mycenaeans were strong enough to occupy Knossos and to dominate its neighbourhood; what might induce them to lay wholly waste and desolate the island in which they were now to live, and which they could now control? Cretan towns and palaces were not fortified, and the Cretans were not a warlike people. If you could take Knossos, you could take Mallia easily enough. Nirou Khani was a delightful house to live in; why raze it to the ground? Why burn the comfortable villa at Amnisos, the grand mansions at Tylissos, so close to Knossos? Why not leave the farmers and craftsmen of Gournia in peace and take the profits of their trade? Whatever could be the point of destroying this harmless little village? Or Palaekastro, or Pseira? I find it hard to reconcile this theory with the magnitude of the catastrophe, its wide extent, and in most places its finality. If this were the best we could do, it would be better to do something else.

If not man, then nature; and that means, in the circumstances, earthquake or the consequences of volcanic activity.

Earthquake alone, independent of volcanic activity, is not a probable answer to our question. Earthquake might account for the destruction, but it could not account for the abandonment. In ancient as in modern times destruction by earthquake, however damaging, is soon followed by re-building and re-occupation. The land remains fertile, the sea abounds in fish; most people survive, and not all buildings are destroyed. It is doubtful whether earthquake has ever resulted in desolation on the scale attested for Minoan Crete in this period. We are only guessing; and I suppose nobody could positively refute the man who guesses either human agency or earthquake, just that and nothing else. But the truth is that I have no interest in this guesswork; if there were nothing to do but guess, I should be dealing with some other subject. We can make no progress without more facts; and there exists another fact, a large and solid-seeming one. I hasten now to welcome and embrace it.

At some time in the Late Minoan period the volcano at Santorini, about sixty five miles north of Crete, disintegrated after one (or more) of the biggest explosions of which earth-history has left any record. Let us visit the volcano and ask for its advice and help.

[36]Hood[1] 106; Marinatos[1] 18 ff.; Platon[1] 197 f.,[2] 167; Pendlebury 180, 228; Vermeule, *GBA* 143 ff.; Hutchinson 300 ff.
[37]Levi 263.

II Santorini: The Volcano

It seemed best to start by asking certain questions about the ruined palaces and towns of Minoan Crete: what was the apparent cause of destruction in each place; whether destruction was followed by abandonment; whether all or most of the places were destroyed within a short space of time, and, if so, what time it was. The answers to these questions seemed to justify continuing the inquiry. There was much to support, and nothing to contradict, the conclusion that the greater part of the eastern half of Crete was destroyed and abandoned within a short space of time, perhaps about the middle of the fifteenth century B.C. It seemed likely too that the destruction and abandonment were caused by natural, not human, agency. We cannot be sure of this conclusion. It seemed probable; it was not certain. But if now there should appear to have been, within this period, a natural catastrophe of which the destruction and abandonment of the eastern half of Crete would be an understandable consequence, the degree of probability will appear so much the greater. We shall now therefore visit a volcano, the island called Santorini by men, Thera by the gods. It lies about sixty-five miles as the crow flies north of Crete.

Santorini is the crater of a volcano; actually in the past, as potentially in the future, one of the most violent volcanoes in the history of the earth since the last ice-age. *Plate 5a*

The crater-wall is broken in three places. You sail through one of the breaches into a circle of sea. The crater-face and the included sea are called the *caldera*, or cauldron. Much of the sea-bed lies 600-1000 feet deep. The crater-walls are very old, but the volcano is still active in the depths. It is slowly filling up the *caldera*. The centre of activity today is the lava island called Néa Kaïménê. The volcano erupted violently in 1707, 1866, and 1926; it was active on a smaller scale in 1939-41 and 1950-1. *Plate 5b*

Plate 5c

At the present time there is no activity visible except a number of fumaroles emitting small clouds of gas. Néa Kaïménê is the upper part of a volcano-cone which rises about three hundred metres from the sea-bed. The part above sea-level has already reached a height of one hundred and thirty-three metres, occupying about one and a half square kilometres of the surface. The volcano needs some tens (or scores) of thousands of years to complete what is in progress—the filling up of the *caldera* with a new lava-mountain, ready in the fulness of time for another eruption of unimaginable violence.

The broken circle of the crater; the colours of sea and sky; colours and shapes in the crater-wall; white houses and chapels perched on the crater-rim—these all together compose a scene of unforgettable beauty; but Santorini is a dangerous place, and part of its fascination is one's awareness of the menace that is always there. The horrors of the most recent shaking of the crater-wall are still plainly imprinted in ruined houses tumbling down the steep cliffs at Phira and Skaros: on 9 July 1926 two thousand buildings collapsed in forty-five seconds. *Plate C1-2* *Plate D1-2*

Now look more closely at the inner face of the crater. Its height varies; seldom less than 250 feet, generally between 400 and 800, 1100 at the highest point. The principal way up is at the chief town, Phira, where a zig-zag road leads up the steep cliff. The rise from sea to summit here is about 800 feet (1450 normal strides; thirty minutes at leisure, half that in a hurry). The cliff is mostly volcanic rock of various types and ages, but the topmost stratum for long reaches is a thick band of pumice and ash. Much of Santorini and Therasia, and the whole of Aspronisi, are covered by a deep layer of *tephra*.[1] *Plate 5d*

Fig. 8

---

[1] 'Tephra' is a term which includes both pumice and ash. As it is important to distinguish between the pumice and the ash at Santorini, I have as a rule avoided the word.

II SANTORINI: THE VOLCANO

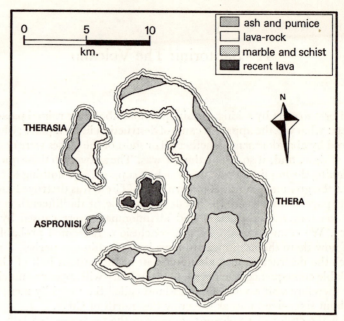

Fig. 8   Santorini: distribution of the tephra-layer

Plate 6a
Plate 6b

The inner face of the crater is so high and steep that you cannot as a rule get near the face of the ash-layer. The easiest place for a close view is in the quarries at Phira, where the ash-cliff has been cut back from the crater-edge. On the south and east coasts, where the ash-layer sits on the ground at sea-level, access is easy.

There is nothing quite like this elsewhere in the world. After the erosion of 3500 years the layer of pumice and ash lies a hundred feet deep over large areas, and depths of a hundred and fifty feet and more have been measured in some places.

This huge downpour of pumice and ash plays, or may play, a leading part in the tragedy of Minoan Crete. We shall need to remember a few facts about it.

First, the mantle is not uniform from top to bottom. Three phases of activity are plainly distinguishable in some areas:—

Cover

(a) Resting on the lava-bedrock is a layer of almost pure pumice, sometimes pink, generally 12-15 feet thick.

(b) Above this lies a distinctive 'coloured-ribbon' layer, consisting of narrow bands of pink or white ash and gray or white pumice; the thicker bands form a layer generally about four feet thick, but thinner bands less distinctly stratified extend further upwards.

(c) Above the 'coloured-ribbon' layer lies a huge deposit of white volcanic ash.

Fig. 9

These strata represent distinguishable phases of volcanic activity. First, the ejection of masses of almost pure pumice; secondly, a number of smaller eruptions depositing the 'coloured-ribbon' layers; thirdly and finally, a paroxysmic eruption which blew out a large part of the volcano's interior in the form of volcanic ash. What is unfortunately not so plain is the answer to the question whether these three phases all occurred within a short space of time (days, weeks, months, at most a year or two) or were spread out over a relatively long period (say, a decade or two). And this is a question of the greatest importance to the present inquiry. We shall see, later on, that the archaeological evidence indicates a quite long interval between the destruction of buildings under the pumice-layer on Santorini and the destruction of the towns and palaces in Minoan Crete. The culture of the latter is distinctly more advanced than that of the former. If all the strata

14

Plate A1 Zakro, the palace

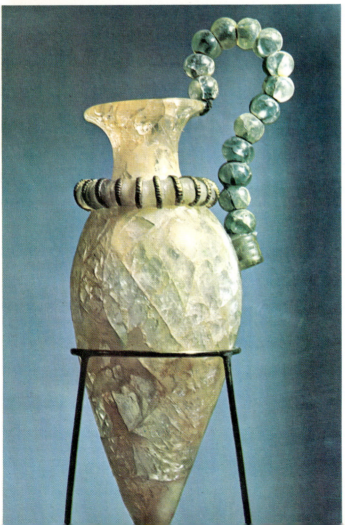

Plate A2 Zakro, rock-crystal ritual vessel

Plate B1   Zakro, stone vase with wild goat

Plate B2   Zakro, bull's head of black chlorite

Plate C1   Santorini, looking across from Phira to Therasia

Plate C2   Santorini, the northern tip of the crescent

Plate D1 Santorini, looking north from Skaros

Plate D2 Santorini, the crater face and houses on the rim

II SANTORINI: THE VOLCANO

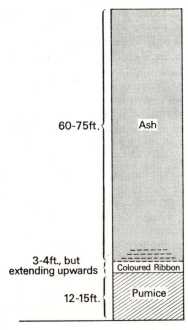

Fig. 9 Santorini: stratification of the tephra-layer

represent a single eruptive phase, to be reckoned in days or weeks or months, the relation of the volcano's activity to the destruction of Crete becomes incomprehensible. We are going to need at least a decade or two between the great fall of pumice which destroyed all life on Santorini and the huge fall of ash which could have rendered Crete uninhabitable.

Erosion on the surface of the pumice-layer indicates an interval between that layer and what lies above it. The leading authorities on the vulcanology of Santorini, Reck and Georgalas, maintain that the interval between the great pumice-layer and the great ash-layer may be quite long[2]—decades, possibly, according to Professor Georgalas;[3] and we are very glad to hear him say so. But others[4] are confident that the visible phenomena require not more than days or at most weeks; and they give us no pleasure, but much pain. For (I repeat) if we are going to connect the desolation of Crete with the action of the volcano, we shall need at least a couple of decades between the fall of the pumice and the fall of the ash.

Plate 6c

The second fact to remember is that the lava-bedrock on which the pumice rests is weathered, and humus had formed on it; that is to say, the surface of Santorini had not been seriously disturbed by volcanic action for a very long time when the pumice fell.

Thirdly, we observe a huge deposit of pumice and ash and a disintegrated mountain; what is the relation between these two phenomena? The French vulcanologist Fouqué gave the correct answer a hundred years ago: the ejection of enormous masses of pumice and ash and the disintegration of the mountain are successive and causally connected phases of one and the same eruptive process. I describe it briefly.

The material ejected in a volcanic eruption consists of 'magma'—molten rock charged with gases. Magma issues from the volcano mainly in two ways: by flowing as a stream of lava; or by violent ejection in the form of bombs, pumice, and ash. Volcanic bombs are lumps of magma ejected and solidified as lava in passage through the air. The great bulk of the material violently ejected upwards consists of pumice and ash. Pumice is the froth on

[2]Reck i 122 f.   [3]At the Thera Congress.   [4]At the Thera Congress.

II SANTORINI: THE VOLCANO

top of the magma; when the gas-content of the magma is very high, the surface turns to froth as the magma rises up the cone into zones of decreasing pressure, and the frothy surface is blown upwards in the form of pumice. Volcanic ash is pumice reduced to minute particles, consisting mainly of glass. According to Ninkovich and Heezen the Santorini ash is '95% colourless volcanic glass'.

The two phenomena visible at Santorini, the ejection of huge masses of pumice and ash and the annihilation of the volcano-cone, leaving a crater-ring miles wide surrounding a deep depression, have a number of parallels both ancient and modern. At Crater Lake in Oregon, for example, there was once a mountain 12,000 feet high. All that is visible today is a crater 500-2000 feet high surrounding a lake six miles across and 2000 feet deep. Seventeen cubic miles of rock are missing; where are they? Ejected pumice and ash will hardly account for a third of the bulk. At Santorini, as at Crater Lake, there is nothing to be seen but pumice and ash resting on weathered and therefore much older rock surrounding a wide and deep depression; where is the rest of the ancient cone, some cubic miles of it? There is hardly any trace of it; and that means that the mountain must have collapsed downwards and inwards, not upwards and outwards. The process was similar at Tambora in Indonesia in 1815, at Coseguina in Nicaragua in 1835, and at Cracatoa in the Sunda Straits in 1883. The interior of the mountain is evacuated by colossal ejections of molten rock reduced to pumice and ash. When the evacuation has gone far enough, the mountain-walls become too thin to stand unsupported; the upper part of the mountain collapses, inwards, into what is now, at Crater Lake and Santorini, the enclosed water. The process was recently described by a vulcanologist in the following terms. 'The rapid draining of the magma-chambers . . . by the ejection of tremendous quantities of pumice and ash . . . leaves the upper part of the cone without support, and its summit collapses . . . [It] creates an empty space in the magma-chamber into which the upper part of the cone collapses'.[5]

Fig. 10

These matters are strictly relevant, indeed indispensable, to the study of the relation between the volcano at Santorini and the desolation of Minoan Crete. It is essential to establish that the volcanic activity was of this and not of some other type. For this is the only type of volcanic eruption which may cause destruction at a great distance from its centre. And Santorini is indeed a classic example of the type; visible here are the huge deposit of pumice and ash and the disintegrated volcano.

Destruction at a great distance may be caused by this type of volcano in two ways. (1) Vast quantities of ash are ejected to a great height. Much of this is carried by high-altitude winds, accelerated by the volcanic fire-storm; and the ash is deposited on land that lies under the track of the winds. (2) Big sea-floods are generated, mainly by the raising of the sea-bed, but also by the disturbance of the sea-level which accompanies the collapse of the volcano-cone and the breach of the crater.

The magnitude of the final paroxysm at Santorini—that which left the great ash-layer and broke the mountain down—was such that a land so close as Crete will have been severely damaged if it lay in the path of the ash-cloud and the sea-floods; whether it did so lie we shall inquire later. Meantime, in order to appreciate the magnitude of the final paroxysm we must contemplate a few facts and figures.

The area enclosed by the crater-ring at Santorini is about 83 square kilometres. Below sea-level the depth inside the crater is generally between 200 and 300 metres. The total volume displaced cannot be calculated, because we do not know how high the mountain rose; modern estimates vary within very wide limits, from 400 m. to 2000 m. It is in any case certain that the volume of rock displaced at Santorini was much greater than in other volcanic eruptions from that day to this, except perhaps in the eruption of Tambora, on an island east of Java, in 1815. It is generally said that the biggest eruption of historical times is that of Cracatoa in 1883. Now the *caldera* at Cracatoa is 23 square kilometres—little more than a quarter the size of Santorini's; and the highest point of Cracatoa before

[5]Bullard 72.

16

II SANTORINI: THE VOLCANO

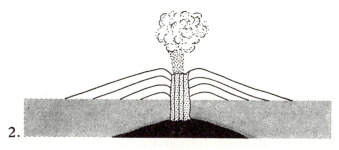

Fig. 10   Stages in the development of a caldera

II SANTORINI: THE VOLCANO

the eruption, 2623 feet, was most probably not higher than that of Santorini, probably indeed lower. In volume of material displaced and ejected Santorini multiplies Cracatoa by at least four and perhaps by more.

Cracatoa has much in common with Santorini. Both volcanoes are islands. In both places the ejection of immense quantities of pumice and ash terminated in the collapse of the cone and the formation of a *caldera* as described above.

Five years after the eruption of Cracatoa the Royal Society published a monumental report, compiled by scientists commissioned to investigate various aspects of the event. One or two of the lessons to be learnt from this report have been generally or even wholly neglected. I therefore report some of the facts afresh.[6]

The paroxysmic phase at Cracatoa lasted a hundred days.[7] On 20 May 1883 the volcano began to boom. Doors and windows rattled at a distance of a hundred miles. Two days later a column of ash rose seven miles high, and falls of ash were observed at a distance of three hundred miles. Throughout June and July and the greater part of August the activity continued, with numerous earthquakes and explosions. On 26 August, from mid-day onwards, the ash-column rose to seventeen miles, and there was a series of exceptionally violent explosions, heard all through the island of Java. 'From sunset till midnight there was an almost continuous roar'. The violence declined for a few hours after midnight; but then, from 05.30 to 10.52 on the morning of the 27th, there were four stupendous eruptions, and Cracatoa disintegrated. The third of these four explosions, at 10.02, was by very far the loudest noise ever recorded on earth. It was heard as far west as the island of Rodriguez, 3080 miles away, and as far east as Alice Springs in Australia, 2233 miles away.[8] From 19.00 till 23.00 there were further explosions, then a decline; the last explosion occurred at 02.30 on the following morning.

The eruption of Cracatoa was over, but not its consequences. Wind-borne ash fell at a distance of 3300 miles; sea-borne pumice spread over scores of thousands of square miles. Tides rose on very remote shores: at Colombo in Ceylon, fifteen inches above the previous highest; seventeen inches at Port Alfred in South Africa, 4500 miles away; seven inches at Cape Horn, over 7000 miles from Cracatoa.[9] Air-waves passed three and a half times round the earth at a speed of over 700 miles an hour.[10] Particles of ash retained in the upper atmosphere created unusual celestial phenomena all round the world for many months—suns rising green, then turning blue; green moons and blue moons; solar and lunar haloes; auroras in unlikely latitudes.[11]

But our concern is rather with the local phenomena. What happens to adjacent lands within a radius of seventy or eighty miles when a volcano of this type erupts so violently? I shall not repeat the tale of the more temporary damages and distresses: panic, as if the end of the world had come; darkness by day for fifty-seven hours up to a radius of fifty miles; walls cracking and windows exploding at a distance of a hundred miles; hot ash and pumice raining down; streams and wells choked, plantations ruined. There are many contemporary accounts, some of them most vivid and moving.[12] I focus attention for a moment on a quite different aspect—the fact that serious damage was confined to a narrow strip of coast on either side of the volcanic centre. The main land-masses of Java and Sumatra suffered little. A couple of months later there was not much trace of the eruptions to be seen on land except on the coastal fringes. There, and there only, life was destroyed and lands devastated; not by the materials ejected, but by sea-floods generated by the eruption.

Before we look more closely at the sea-floods, let us ask a question about the only other possible source of lasting damage to the land—the downpour of enormous quantities of

---

[6]In what follows I have relied mainly on the Royal Society Report; the best general account in recent years, with substantial bibliography, is that of Furneaux.
[7]*RS* 11 ff.   [8]*RS* 80 f.   [9]*RS*, Tables following p. 148.
[10]*RS* 57 ff.   [11]*RS* 152 ff.   [12]Furneaux quotes many.

II SANTORINI: THE VOLCANO

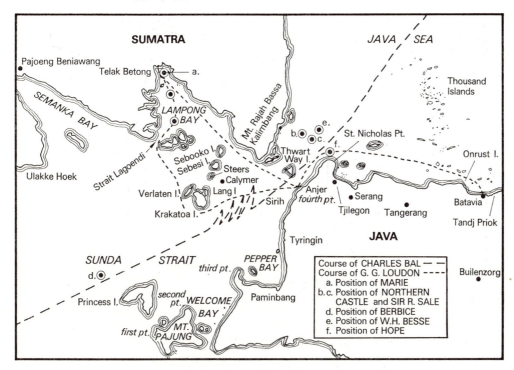

Fig. 11   Cracatoa and the adjacent coasts

pumice and ash. Several cubic miles of this went up; all but a small fraction came down again. Where did it fall, and in what depth? There are one or two facts to be remembered when we return to Crete.

The damage done by ash-fall to the land on either side of the Sunda Straits was slight. At Batavia, 94 miles away, the downpour on the final day lasted about five hours; at Buitenzorg, 100 miles away, about three hours.[13] The deposit was thin; the mainlands were washed clean by the rains of the monsoon months which followed. In Sumatra, to the north-west, the ash-fall reached to a distance of 330 miles but was thin everywhere except on the coast facing the volcano; the only depth I have seen recorded far inland is 22 millimetres.

Where, then, did the huge masses fall? They fell in two different types of area. First, on and about the volcano. A vast volume fell more or less straight down, the density diminishing as the distance from the volcano increased. The volcanic centre was covered with a layer 200-250 feet deep in places; on the periphery, the layer on Verlaten Island was 100 feet deep; forty miles to the north, the rate of deposit on the decks of *Governor-General Loudon* was three feet an hour;[14] sixty-six miles north of the volcano, *Norham Castle* measured eighteen inches in an hour.[15]

But that is only part, the least important part, of the story. The column of ash from Cracatoa on the final day rose to a height of at least thirty (some say fifty) miles; and the great bulk of the topmost miles was carried by violent winds along a particular path to the south-west. The ash-cloud spread over a vast triangle, the density of the downpour diminishing as the distance increased. We shall need particularly to inquire whether Crete lay under the path of wind-borne ash from Santorini; if it did, we shall be quite sure that Crete must have been covered in a deep layer of ash. Remember, now and always, that Santorini

Fig. 11

Fig. 12

[13]*RS* 26 f.   [14]*RS* 27.   [15]*RS* 269.

II SANTORINI: THE VOLCANO

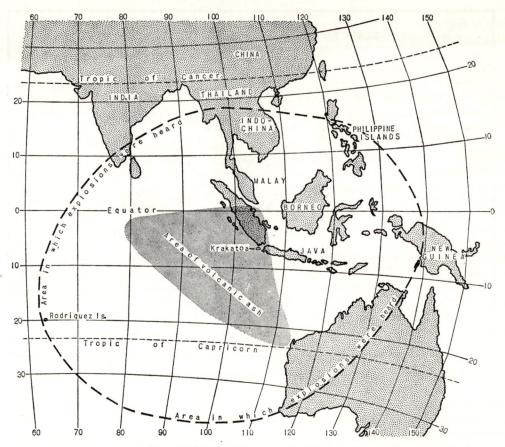

Fig. 12 Cracatoa: the area of the ash-deposit

far surpasses Cracatoa in volume of material ejected; and that the distance from Santorini to Crete is about the same as the distance of *Norham Castle* from Cracatoa—sixty-six miles.

The wind-borne ash-cloud from Cracatoa was still raining twelve days later at a distance of 3300 miles.[16] It seems likely that a deep deposit would have been left on land within seventy or eighty miles south or south-west of Cracatoa. As it happens, there is no land at these distances in these directions. Indeed, excepting the little Christmas and Cocos Islands, there is no land within two thousand miles along the path taken by the ash-cloud from Cracatoa. There is therefore no direct evidence of the depth of the deposit on land along the storm-path at a distance that would be relevant to Crete; but there is abundant evidence about the duration of the ash-fall, and some about its depth, at a series of much greater distances.

I give a few out of a large number of examples from the log-books of ships caught in the ash-storm.[17] At 370 miles, *Tweed* measured seven inches on her decks; at 830 miles, *Castleton* recorded that the air was loaded with ash which fell in great quantities for twelve hours; at 900 miles, *Earl of Beaconsfield* reported a very heavy fall of ash for four days; at about 1000 miles, *Brani* logged a vast quantity falling for eleven hours; in the same area, heavy showers of ash fell on *Lennox Castle* for four days; at 1127 miles, *Arabella* recorded a continuous fall for two days; at 1160 miles, *Simla* ran through a continuous ash-fall for

[16] *RS* 281.

[17] *RS* 264 ff., 447 f.

II SANTORINI: THE VOLCANO

two days; and at the prodigious distance of 3313 miles from Cracatoa, from the 6th to the 8th of September (ten to twelve days after the eruptions) *Scotia* logged a slight but continuous fall of ash. All these vessels lay under the path taken by the wind-borne ash-cloud to the west of Cracatoa. It seems a likely inference that a land-area within seventy or eighty miles of Cracatoa lying under the storm-path would have been covered with ash to a depth to be measured in yards. We have already noted that *Norham Castle*, sixty-six miles from the volcano and lying to windward, measured a foot and a half in an hour.

So much for the ash-fall; I return to the sea-floods. These also have something to teach us, worth remembering when we return to Crete.[18]

The first big wave reached the Java coast at Tyringin, twenty-four miles from Cracatoa, between 18.00 and 19.00 on 26 August (the day before the final paroxysm). It destroyed many houses near the coast. Within an hour, another wave swept away a Chinese camp at Merak. No further wave is recorded until 01.00 on 27 August, when Sirik, six miles south of Anjer, was submerged; it is worth noticing that nothing was observed at Anjer itself at this time. The first enormous killer-wave arrived at Anjer at 06.30 on the final day; it swept away almost the whole harbour-town. An hour later a second gigantic wave completed the destruction of Anjer and submerged part of Telok Betong. These two big waves correspond to the first two big eruptions of that morning, the first at 05.30 and the second at 06.44. The third and biggest eruption, at 10.02, was followed by an enormous wave which flooded the coastal fringes of Java and Sumatra and carried away what was left of Tyringin, Merak, and Telok Betong, as well as many other settlements on the shores. All vessels on or close to the coasts were sunk or stranded; but vessels sailing in the Straits did not even notice the passing of the great wave beneath them.

Estimates of the height of the wave on arrival at the coast vary according to place and observer; for most places, fifty feet is a fair guess. At Merak, where the wave poured up a narrow inlet, the flood rose to at least a hundred feet. The greatest height to which the water certainly reached inland was 115 feet; the greatest height at which buildings were swept away was 47 feet.

The speed of the waves between Cracatoa and the coasts is not known. The books give figures; but the time of arrival of waves within the Straits was nowhere precisely recorded.[19] For precise recording we have to go further afield: to Batavia, which the flood-wave (only six feet high) reached in $2\frac{1}{2}$ hours, having travelled 100 miles over a mean depth of 180 feet at 40 m.p.h.; and to North Watcher Island, which the waves (not more than eight feet high) reached in $1\frac{1}{2}$ hours, having travelled 82 miles over a mean depth of 66 feet at 54 m.p.h.

These two places, Batavia and North Watcher Island, lie beyond the eastern exit of the Straits; and it is relevant to our purpose to notice two facts. First, that the flood-waves from Cracatoa did not move uniformly in all directions. They broke out mainly to the west, inundating adjacent coasts, rushing through the western exit, and raising tides on shores at enormous distances westwards—in Ceylon, in South Africa, in South America. To the north and east, the flood-waves were insignificant. At North Watcher Island, eighty-two miles away over the open sea to the north, the biggest wave was only eight feet high at the shore. When we return to Crete, we must ask whether there is any reason to believe that the flood-waves from Santorini were directed towards Crete; and we may see some reason to believe that they were not. Secondly, the waves from Cracatoa did not turn corners, at least not in noticeable volume. For example, Vlakke Hoek, directly in the path of the flood-waves, was attacked by a fifty-foot wave thrice at half-hourly intervals; but Benkunat, thirty miles round the corner to the west, noticed nothing, nor did Kroe, thirty miles further away in the same direction. No place on the south coast of Sumatra recorded a wave higher than nine feet, and most recorded much less. If the main flood-waves from Santorini were directed towards the north coast of Crete (and we do not yet

[18]For what follows, see *RS* 89 ff.   [19]*RS* 106, Table I.

II SANTORINI: THE VOLCANO

know whether they were or not), it is not likely that they did much harm to Palaekastro and Zakro, far down the east coast and protected by the extension of Cape Sidhero.

Between 01.00 and 11.00 on 27 August the flood-waves killed 36,380 persons on the coastal fringes of Java and Sumatra adjacent to the volcano.[20] The waves receded quickly, leaving the coastal fringes partly flooded, partly a desolation of mud covered in sea-borne pumice; but recovery was surprisingly rapid. 'Of the areas devastated by ash-fall and sea-floods from Cracatoa, none suffered more than the district of Bantam; yet, within a month . . . , the tropical rains washed away the ash, and fresh green grass re-appeared'.[21] On Cracatoa itself only ten years later 61 species of plants and 132 species of birds and insects were collected.[22]

Such are the principal lessons to be learnt from Cracatoa. When we come to consider whether Crete must have been damaged, and may have been devastated, by the eruption of Santorini, we shall remember the known effects of a much smaller displacement of material in an eruption of the same type. We shall remember the explosion heard 3000 miles away; the tides rising seventeen inches at a distance of 4500 miles; the heavy ash-fall for four days at a distance of 900 miles; the sea-floods fifty feet high on adjacent shores. We shall remember also that both the ash-cloud and the sea-floods followed particular paths, and that the sea-floods did not turn corners. We shall remember how quickly the worst-afflicted lands recovered from the disaster. We shall not suppose that Crete might recover so quickly as an area lying six degrees south of the equator; but I mention in passing that Néa Kaïmnéê, the new volcano-peak inside the ancient crater at Santorini, which erupted violently in 1926 and has been active on more than one occasion since, has thirty-four species of plants[23] and one quite tall tree growing.

Cracatoa was not the biggest of the modern eruptions, though it made the loudest noise; I conclude with a word about a much bigger eruption, perhaps as big as that of Santorini. It occurred in 1815 on the island of Sumbawa, about 180 miles east of Java; and it has one or two points of interest to our inquiry.

The volcano called Tambora, believed to be extinct, awoke in 1814. Its paroxysmic phase began on 5 April 1815, and culminated in a series of colossal explosions on 11 and 12 April. About ten cubic miles of rock were ejected in the form of pumice and ash; the collapse of the weakened mountain-walls reduced the height of the volcano from 13,000 to 9,000 feet. The *caldera* thus formed was fifteen miles in circumference—nearly as big as Santorini's.[24]

There was no contemporary or near-contemporary scientific study of this gigantic eruption. Sir Stamford Raffles, Lieutenant-Governor of Java at the time, reported that the biggest explosions were heard at a distance of 900 miles, and that ash lay three feet deep in Java at a place three hundred miles from the volcano.[25] The quantity of volcanic ash retained in the upper atmosphere was so great that the sun's rays were partly absorbed for many months, and the mean world-temperature dropped one degree centigrade in the following year; plant-growth was inhibited, and 1816 was known as 'the year without a summer'.

About 12,000 persons were killed on Sumbawa; and the first point of relevance to us is the fact that the damage caused by ash-fall was so great that at least 50,000 persons—probably many more—died of starvation in the months following the great eruptions. The effect of the ash-fall from Santorini must have been similar in Crete, if Crete lay under the track of the wind-borne ash-cloud.

There is a second point of interest.[26] Although the material displaced was enormously greater in bulk at Tambora than at Cracatoa, the biggest bang from Cracatoa was very much louder than the biggest from Tambora. The reason is that Cracatoa concentrated

[20] RS 26. [21] Furneaux 178 f. [22] Furneaux 188.
[23] Professor C. Diapoulis, to the Thera Congress. [24] Wilcoxson 126 ff.
[25] Wilcoxson 125. [26] RS 447.

Plate 3a Pseira, the town

Plate 3b Mochlos

Plate 3c Phaestos

Plate 3d Mallia

Plate 4a Patterns on LM Ia pottery

Plate 4b Patterns on LM Ib pottery

Plate 4c LM II 'Palace Style' jar, from Knossos

Plate 4d LM I Octopus-flask, from Palaekastro

Plate 5a Santorini, from the air

Plate 5b Santorini, the summit of the active volcano

Plate 5d Santorini, the way up the cliff at Phira

Plate 5c Santorini, the eruption of 1926

Plate 6a Santorini, the face of the ash-layer

Plate 6b Santorini, the face of the ash-layer

Plate 6c Santorini, erosion on the surface of the pumice-layer

Plate 7a Bronze blade with gold-inlay, from Santorini

Plate 7b Acrotiri, the ravine from the south

Plate 7c Acrotiri, the cliffs of pumice and ash

Plate 7d
Acrotiri, the bed of the ravine

Plate 8a   Acrotiri, the angle of a house-wall

Plate 8b   Acrotiri, two walls

Plate 8c   Acrotiri, two walls

Plate 8d   Acrotiri, west-east wall

II SANTORINI: THE VOLCANO

its final convulsions into the short space of five and a half hours, whereas Tambora culminated in a series of more numerous explosions, individually less colossal than Cracatoa's, spread over a much longer time; the explosions from Tambora 'lasted thirty-four days'; they 'accelerated violently from April 5th to April 12th'.[27] We must allow for the possibility that the climax at Santorini was of the Tambora-type, a series of eruptions spread over days or weeks; so that, although the quantity of material displaced remains as great as ever, the sea-floods generated by the various eruptions may not have been so big as is sometimes supposed.

I am eager to return to Crete; but we still need a few more facts, and the place to seek them is under the pumice in Santorini. For when the great mass of pumice fell on the island it buried the well-built houses of men; men who had prospered in their beautiful land; men who had shared the culture of Minoan Crete. It must surely be of interest to go underneath the mantle of pumice and ash, to dig out the buried settlements, and to see what may still be learnt about the men whose homes were on the mountain at Santorini when their world disintegrated.

[27] Wilcoxson 125, quoting Sir Stamford Raffles.

III Santorini: The Buried Town

The building of the Suez Canal began in 1859. An immense quantity of cement was needed, and Santorini was the place to supply it. The deep ash-layer on the islands had four great virtues: a mixture of the ash with lime makes a cement which is exceptionally hard and waterproof; the supply is practically inexhaustible; procurement was easy, for masses of ash could be detached from the cliff-face and tipped down into boats waiting below; and transport was quick and cheap.

Fig. 13 The areas exploited were the west and especially the south coast of Therasia and the little bay of Balos on the main island. At a point about half-way along the south coast of Therasia the ash was cut away until a level was reached where blocks of stone began to impede the work. It was obvious (the workmen knew it at once) that the stones were relics of man-made walls. From 1866 onwards the site was skilfully excavated, first by the mine-owner, M. Alafousos, and a friend, Dr Nomikos, then by the French vulcanologist Fouqué. Their first objective was to determine whether the walls were built before the pumice fell or (as they might have been) placed in a clearing made under pumice already fallen. It was quickly established that the walls had been standing before the pumice fell; the first step towards dating the pumice-fall had been taken.

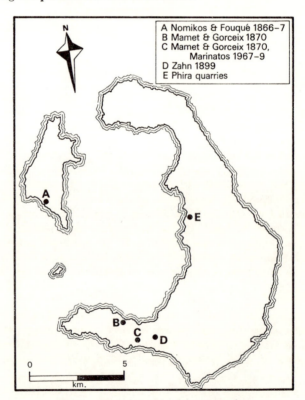

Fig. 13 Santorini: sites of the excavations

III SANTORINI: THE BURIED TOWN

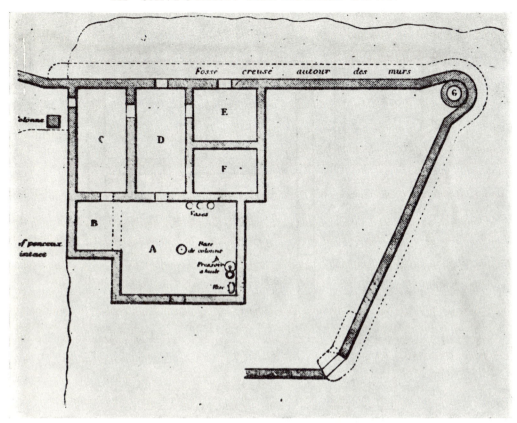

Fig. 14 Excavation on the south coast of Therasia, by M. Fouqué in 1867

1. *Excavation on the south coast of Therasia.*[1]   *Fig. 14*

The ruins (no longer discoverable) were impressive. Room A+B is 8½ m. long; rooms C and D are 6×2.50 m.; E and F, 3.80×3 and 2.50. The so-called 'boundary-wall' runs 8 m. from E to G and turns back southward for 18 m. 'G' is a stone cylinder rising 1 m. above the ground (for whatever purpose). The walls were made of unshaped lava-blocks, mortared with clay and re-inforced with beams of olive with the bark still on. The walls were not plastered or painted. The ceiling was of earth and stone resting on a timber frame. Room A had a central base of stone for a column of wood. All the walls were laid directly on the weathered bedrock of lava. Among the relics were barley and other grains; no metal, but some stone tools; parts of a human skeleton; and much pottery, well-preserved.

In 1870 excavations were conducted by MM. Mamet and Gorceix, of the French School at Athens, on both sides of the coast of Santorini in the region of Acrotiri:

2. *Excavation at Balos.*   *Fig. 15*

On the inner crater-face at Balos, as on Therasia, the cutting of ash was checked when the stripping of the cliff-face reached a layer of stones. These again were plainly walls of dwellings, superior in quality to those of Therasia. The stones were shaped and laid ashlar-style. The inner sides of walls were plastered and painted yellowish. The absence of

---

[1] I follow Fouqué 94-131, with Plates xxxix-xlii; H. Mamet, *de Insula Thera* (1874); Renaudin, *BCH* xlvi (1922) 113 ff.; Zahn's results are briefly published in H. von Gaertringen's *Thera* iii; cf Åberg, *Bronzezeitl. und früheisenzeitl. Chronologie* iv 127 f.

III SANTORINI: THE BURIED TOWN

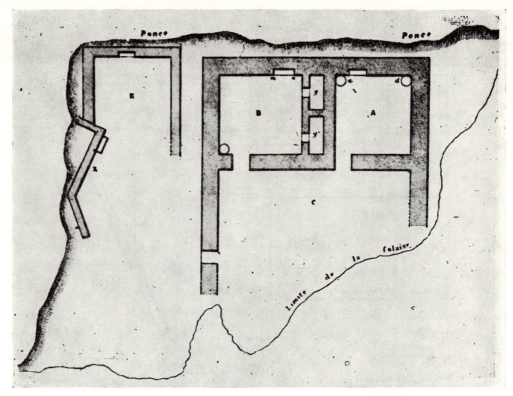

Fig. 15   Excavation at Balos, by MM. Mamet and Gorceix

windows and the nature of the relics on the black-soil floors indicate that the walls belong to service-rooms. Rooms A and B contained large jars holding barley, lentils, and peas. There was a complete skeleton of a goat. Rooms g and g' were for storage of barley and straw. Room E had (among other things) a copper saw and a trunk of olive six feet long with the branches still on it. Obsidian and pottery were abundant. Along the cliff-face beyond the excavated area runs a stratum of similar habitations, and many vases have been found hereabouts.

But the most promising area for excavation was on the other side of Acrotiri, roughly south of the village. The southern and south-western coasts of Santorini are relatively low-lying, with some quite long beaches; and the ash-layer is severly eroded in parts of these regions. There are some places, especially ravines cut by rain and eroded by weathering, where the mantle is reduced to a thin cover or even to nothing at all. Nobody is going to dig down through many metres of ash on the off-chance of finding habitations underneath; but where the mantle is thin there is hope of finding places where walls or other objects appear on the surface.

In 1867 Fouqué explored some of the ravines south of Acrotiri and discovered walls and pottery and sundry other objects. In 1870 Mamet and Gorceix, and in 1899 Robert Zahn, conducted systematic excavations at several points in this neighbourhood. Neither the Frenchmen nor the German published precise information about the location of their sites, and these have not been re-discovered.

Fig. 16   3. *Excavation in a ravine south of Acrotiri* (1).

The walls, 50 cm. thick, are laid directly on the bedrock; they were preserved in part to a

III SANTORINI: THE BURIED TOWN

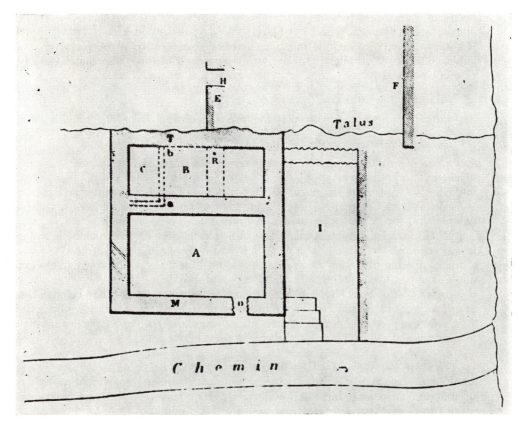

Fig. 16 Excavation in a ravine south of Acrotiri, by M. Fouqué and MM. Mamet and Gorceix

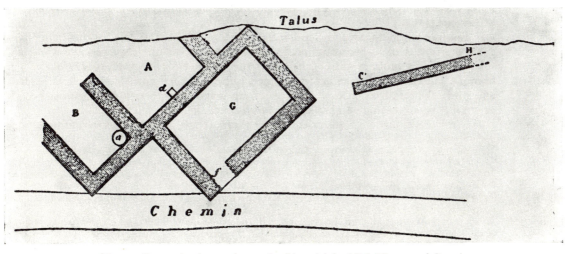

Fig. 17 Excavation in a ravine south of Acrotiri, by MM. Mamet and Gorceix

III SANTORINI: THE BURIED TOWN

height of 2 m. The stones are roughly shaped and laid ashlar-style, clay-mortared. The interior walls of Rooms E and F were plastered and decorated with paintings in a variety of colours. The relics include many animal-bones, especially of sheep and goat; a saw, knives, scrapers of obsidian; mortars, grinders, spindle-whorls; and many vases in near-perfect condition.

Fig. 17

4. *Excavation in a ravine south of Acrotiri* (2).

Both architecture and relics are very like the preceding.

5. *Excavation in a ravine south of Acrotiri* (3).

A complex of buildings, apparently store-rooms. The contents added numerous items to the inventory: a circular trinket of gold; traces of fishing-nets; bones of pig, dog, donkey (or mule); evidence for pressing of olives and grinding of grain; coriander and anise as well as barley and chick-pea; the rim of a jar with a 'Linear A' inscription; a great deal of pottery; and finally one object which deserves a paragraph to itself.

Plate 7a
The illustration shows a bronze blade with gold-inlay of shapely and mobile battle-axes.[2] It was acquired by Robert Zahn in 1899 from the owner of a vineyard at Potamos, close to the excavation-site.[3] It is the product of a difficult technique,[4] represented in Crete by a single example, by a small number in Greece and the islands. The process of manufacture is complex and delicate. Such blades are articles of great value. They belonged to royal or at least very grand persons, not to ordinary men; and it was natural to infer from this little relic the presence of a great man in Santorini and the existence, somewhere under the pumice and ash, of his palatial dwelling on the island.

This was the state of affairs at the beginning of the present century. The sum of knowledge was already quite large. The pumice fell on a comfortable and prosperous community. There were farmers, foresters, weavers, masons, potters, and fishermen; gold, copper, and obsidian were imported from overseas; buildings were solid and stylish, not without luxury. And already there was a likely answer to the question 'when did the pumice fall?' Excavation and chance-finds indicated that the pumice fell during a period of culture which in Crete is called 'Late Minoan I a'.

We have had to wait a long time, sixty-eight years, for a renewal of the attempt to resurrect this 'new Pompeii', as Fouqué called it. For the past three summers, beginning in June 1967, Professor Marinatos has been excavating a site on the main island.[5] The scene of the excavation is a ravine leading to the sea about ten minutes' walk south of the village *Plates 7b–d* of Acrotiri.

Erosion has reduced the depth of the deposit along the line of the ravine-path generally to a shallow bed of pumice above the ruins; but the depth increases on both sides of the path, and the walls of the ravine rise (in the east, abruptly) to a height of 5 m. or more. The ruins are buried in pure pumice. Excavation in pumice has its own difficulties, and protection of all excavated parts from rain is indispensable. The difficulties become very great when the high embankments are reached.

My present purpose is historical rather than archaeological; I ask certain questions,

---

[2]Vermeule, *GBA* pl. 13C=Perrot & Chipiez, *Histoire de l'art* vi fig. 212; Luce, pl. 43.

[3]The provenance of the blade is not known precisely. *Thera* iii fig. 29 shows the site of Zahn's excavation in the 'Thal des Potamos', and we are told (p. 40) that the blade came into Zahn's possession 'von dem Besitzer des Weinberges am Potamos'; it was a 'kleine Bronzeklinge, die in dem Hause dort gefunden war'.

[4]Vermeule *GBA* 98; Marinatos[1] 104, 167; Karo, *Schachtgraeber* 313; Evans *PM* iii 113; Hutchinson 249; Platon[1] 168.

[5]I must make it plain that the materials on which the remainder of this lecture is based are the property of Professor Marinatos, the discoverer of the site and the director of its excavation from the beginning. I depend wholly on his publications and on what I learnt from him on the site in 1968 and 1969, when my wife and I had the great privilege of Professor Marinatos' company and instruction.

III SANTORINI: THE BURIED TOWN

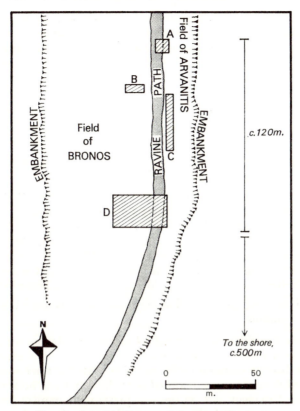

Fig. 18 Acrotiri: diagram of the excavation-area

and show illustrations as evidence of the answers I give. What exactly has Professor Marinatos found? What sort of place is it? What is the date of the settlement? What is its relation to Minoan Crete? What can be learnt about its history?

First, a word about the extent of the settlement. The diagram shows the four principal areas of excavation (named after the owners of the land); it does not show tunnellings into the embankments or smaller trenchings and soundings, all of which have been productive. It will be seen that the present excavations lie within a small area, about 120 m. long and 50 m. broad; but it is already certain that the ruins extend both north and south and into the embankments on both sides. It seems probable that this was a large settlement; and it may have been very large, for it may have extended east as far as the site excavated by Zahn, about a thousand yards distant, and possibly as far north as the site excavated by Mamet and Gorceix, about two thousand yards distant.

Fig. 18

Secondly, what kind of buildings are being uncovered at Acrotiri? The answer is, in broad terms, the mansions of grand or at least very prosperous persons. It seems at present very probable that what is emerging from the pumice is not a royal palace like Mallia or Zakro, and certainly not an unpretentious village like Pseira or Gournia; rather it is another Tylissos, a group of costly and massive residences. The evidence for this is as follows:—

(a) First, the quality of the masonry. Plate 8a shows the angle of a house-wall, including doorway. This is ashlar stone-work of high quality. Plate 8b shows, on the right, the end of a massive and well-built wall which runs 14 m. from north to south. A gap of a few feet separates it from another wall, 2 m. high, running from west to east 5 m. long before it

Plate 8a
Plate 8b

29

III SANTORINI: THE BURIED TOWN

Plate 8d
Plate 8c
disappears into the embankment. The stones of this wall are brittle, presumably through the heat of the falling pumice. Plate 8c shows the same two walls as they appeared in September 1969; and Plate 8d gives a closer view of the wall which runs west-east into the embankment.

Stone-work of this quality proves the presence not only of first-class masons but also of ambitious architects and wealthy clients. The work is not much inferior in quality to that of the great mansions in contemporary Crete.

(b) *Wall-paintings.* Wall-painting in a house of this period reflects material prosperity as well as artistic taste. Fragments of painted plaster are very abundant in certain areas:—

Plate 9a
Plate 9a: Head and shoulders of a monkey; white muzzle, blue crown, brown eye. The oval object on the left is presumably foliage.

Plate 9b
Plate 9b: A lively bird, flying; blue head and beak; red throat; wing extended.

Plate 9c
Plate 9c: Head of a man bowing forward towards a palm-tree which seems to be bowing towards him. The man is beardless, with short curly hair; snub-ended nose, thick-lips, large eyebrow. His mouth is open, if only we could hear what he is saying; perhaps a prayer. Two strands of hair float back from his head; ribbons, according to Marinatos. He has a large golden ring in his ear. He looks not at all like a Cretan, not much like a Mycenaean Greek; but I doubt if he is an African, let alone a Bedouin.[6]

Another wall-painting shows an altar surmounted by Minoan horns of consecration and supported by columns.

(c) *Size.* The length, breadth, and height of a building are obvious tokens of grandeur. It was not yet possible in 1969 to define the complete extent of any mansion, but it has been known since 1968 that the mansion in 'Bronos 2' consisted of three storeys.

Plate 9d
Plate 10a
The flagstoned floor shown in Plate 9d is buckled but not broken through. Underneath this floor is a basement, not yet opened, presumably more or less intact. The basement has a window at street-level. (Plate 10a; the flagstoned floor is behind the wall, a little above the level of the window.)

The flagstoned floor has a central column-base. The wooden column which stood on it supported a ceiling, not a roof. This is proved by the contents of the room, which include pottery lying high above the floor; it must have fallen from an upper floor. It is thus certain that there were three storeys—the basement; the room with the flagstoned floor; and the room supported by the central column.

(d) *Interior stone-staircases.* Staircases of stone also are associated with the mansions of the grand.

Plate 10b
Plate 10b shows an interior service-stair of stone in two flights; nine steps are preserved. 'Of no architectural pretensions', as Marinatos says, but well-built and shapely enough.

(e) *The contents.* There follow illustrations of a few specimens of the pottery found in great abundance on the site. It is to be stressed that these are the discards, things not worth taking when the residents left their homes. For it is certain that they had time to leave, and that they took with them all precious and utensil metals, all other objects which they valued. At Pompeii about two thousand human skeletons were found in the pumice; at Acrotiri so far not so much as a single human bone. The discards are of good quality. They include many fine pieces brought oversea from Crete. The number of vessels for use in kitchen and larder of a single house is enormous.

Plate 11a
Plate 11a: A strainer decorated with continuous spirals.

Plate 11b
Plate 11b: A vessel of miniature bath-tub shape decorated with flying swallows.

[6]See *Archaeological Reports for 1968-9* 29.

III SANTORINI: THE BURIED TOWN

The context in which it was found (together with other plainly ritual vessels) favours Marinatos' suggestion that this is a ritual-dish used in celebrating the return of spring.

Plate 11*c*: A polychrome jug decorated with flying swallows. The body is mainly black, with red-brown throat and a large white patch on the back. The tail is divided and very long. *Plate 11c*

Plate 11*d*: Another miniature bath-tub. Dolphins leaping; clouds above, waves below. This elegant dish is of local manufacture. *Plate 11d*

Plate 12*a*: One of many spherical jugs with longish spout. *Plate 12a*

Plate 12*b*: Another, covered with bands of myrtle and ivy-leaves. Local imitation of Cretan ware, not wholly successful (I suppose the bands were meant to be horizontal); it is nevertheless quite a pretty thing. *Plate 12b*

Plate 12*c*: The clay and colours of better quality than usual. *Plate 12c*

Plate 12*d*: The elegant goblets to left and right are imports from Crete; the cup in the middle is local. *Plate 12d*

Plate 13*a*: The bottom of this pot is pierced like a colander. It is one of the most stylistically advanced pieces found so far. *Plate 13a*

Plate 13*b*: A fine piece, imported from Crete. The pendent sprays may be capers. *Plate 13b*

Plate 13*c*: Another import of great elegance; reed-like plants. *Plate 13c*

Pottery is by far the most abundant, though not the only, source of evidence for the date of destruction of the site. Several thousand vases (wholly or in part) have been recovered, a volume large enough to justify generalization even at this early date. Their testimony is clear and is confirmed by other objects, notably by the wall-paintings and by signs in the 'Linear A' script. *Plate 13d*

Imports from Crete include nothing later than the styles and techniques of the mature phase of Late Minoan I a. The native wares are all of the same period. The absolute date of the latest pottery will be not far from 1500 B.C. There is no example of the characteristics by which Late Minoan I b is distinguished from I a; not a single piece to keep company with a certain vessel in the Marine Style of I b, in the German Institute, said to have come from Santorini. If the next few thousand vases from Acrotiri tell the same story, we shall be fairly confident that that vessel came from some other place.

This conclusion, that the pumice-fall destroyed the Santorini settlements in Late Minoan I a, makes our task much harder. For the pottery characteristic of the destruction-levels in the Cretan places is of a distinctly later type. We seem to be absolutely obliged to infer an interval of at least a decade or two between the destruction at Santorini and the destruction in Crete; but such eminent vulcanologists as Yagi, Healy, and Thorarinsson are going to tell us that volcanic eruptions of this type and on this scale occur not in two widely separated phases but in a single phase after a very long period of quiescence. It is no good pleading that Santorini might have developed more slowly than Crete, so that I a in Santorini might be contemporary with I b in Crete; the Cretan imports themselves are all of I a, and nobody is likely to be convinced by the argument that (for whatever reason) all import from Crete was stopped for (say) twenty years before the eruption. I suppose a note of caution should be sounded; excavation has a long way to go yet. But the statistical probabilities against a change in the picture are enormous. Some thousands of witnesses are already in court, testifying that the pumice-fall in Santorini preceded the destruction and desolation of Crete by at least a decade or two.

About the history of the site, no more than a few chapter-headings can be written at present.

1. There is not at present any evidence of buildings of any Minoan period earlier than that of the buildings which are now emerging from the pumice. Where the limit of founda-

III SANTORINI: THE BURIED TOWN

tions has been reached, the stones rest either on bedrock or on soil above it. Moreover, there is not (so far as I know) much evidence of artefacts earlier than Late Minoan I a associated with these buildings. Further excavation may modify the picture; but the picture at present (quite a large one) is of habitations built and furnished in the period of their destruction, Late Minoan I a.

2. The first cause of evacuation of the site was not the pumice-fall; it was earthquake. Evidence of this was observed by Marinatos especially in several places:

Plate 14a   Plate 14*a* shows a doorway in the north wall of a large house. The well-built wall has collapsed in a manner hardly compatible with any other cause but earthquake. Moreover 'the fallen stones' (I quote from Marinatos) 'and the interstices between them were covered with a fine brown earth which was clearly the result of decomposed mud-brick. No trace of pumice exists in this layer'. It is evident that the collapse of this wall and of a mud-brick upper story preceded the fall of the pumice; the pumice lay on top of the debris, not under it or amidst it. The house was already in ruins, reduced to a few courses of stone-wall on the ground-floor, when the pumice fell.

Plate 14b   The west wall of the house, made wholly of rubble, has also collapsed. The holes visible in the pumice are straight and cylindrical; they preserve the shapes of wooden beams caught in the pumice.

Further indications are less convincing in the illustrations than on the site.

Plate 14c   Plate 14*c* shows an area in which large blocks have been thrown some distance from their setting in the wall.

3. In 1969 Marinatos found evidence of a brief period of re-occupation between the destruction by earthquake and the final destruction by the fall of pumice.

Plate 14d   The building illustrated in Plate 14*d* collapsed down to the level of the doorway on the right of the illustration. There are two features to be noticed. First, a crude dry-stone wall has been constructed across the room after the collapse. Secondly, a bath (shown *in situ*) has been placed on a floor laid at a high level inside the room on top of the debris. These two features are alone enough to prove re-occupation of the room after the collapse of the house.

Plate 15a   The entrance to the room was henceforth through what had been its window.

Further evidence is offered by a deliberately blocked flight of stairs. The staircase illus-
Plate 15b trated in Plate 15*b* turned at a right-angle to continue in another flight to an upper floor. Collapse of the upper part of the staircase left a gap which has been filled by a crude continuation upwards of the shattered ground-floor wall.

Plate 15c   The 'Street of the Telchines' is another eloquent witness to earthquake. The house-walls on either side of the street are preserved to ground-floor ceiling-level. The north end of the street was blocked by fallen stones after the earthquake. The present clear access was provided by the re-occupants, who removed the debris from the street and piled it up on
Plate 15d both sides of the end of the street. Plate 15*d* shows the cleared street, and the debris piled up at the end, visible on the left.

It is highly probable that the future will provide more information about this phase of re-occupation. It was a brief and brutish phase, according to Marinatos; the re-occupants were 'squatters', and their tenancy was very short.

Plate 16a   Plate 16*a* looks down into a room occupied by the 'squatters'; simple tools on the floor.

4. Marinatos had noted in 1968 the absence of human skeletons and the lack, or extreme rarity, of portable objects of value. 'The inhabitants', he wrote, 'had ample time and opportunity to take with them everything precious, even metal vessels and tools'. It is now clear that the inhabitants abandoned the site (and presumably left the island) before or immediately after the earthquake. The ruins of their mansions were briefly and uncomfortably occupied by others, perhaps humbler folk whose own homes had been destroyed and who (for whatever reason) remained on the island for a time. As no human remains have been found here, it is probable that the squatters also were driven from the

III SANTORINI: THE BURIED TOWN

island by the growing violence of the volcano. When the great mass of pumice fell, it buried a settlement which had for some time lain in ruins and which was, at the last, wholly or almost wholly deserted. Wholly deserted it remained for hundreds of years.

Let us now look more closely at a particular quarter ('A' in Fig. 18, p. 29), a tripartite store-room. The contents of all three rooms are many and various, including quite a lot that must have descended from upper floors. Clear proof of the collapse of a ceiling is given by the south room: there is the stone base for a wooden column, and, near it, another such column-base evidently fallen from the floor above.

There are lamps, millstones, mortars, tools, weights, vessels of stone as well as clay. Most abundant is the pottery; of local manufacture for the most part, but including some imported pieces. The colours of the painting are well preserved; there has been nothing to damage them since the fall of the pumice. There are no salts or water in the pumice, and the ash which fell later on the pumice admits no water below a couple of metres from its surface. Some of the colours have faded quickly on exposure to air.

I refer briefly to one or two features of the three rooms:—

(*i*) *The south room.* The first great encouragement to the excavator came early in the first season. A row of jars, about three feet tall, emerged from the pumice. Other vessels lay on the floor, oddly cracked, no doubt by heat. *Plate* 16*b* *Plate* 16*c*

(*ii*) *The middle room.* This contained good things, one particularly pleasing; at a certain level above the floor a mass of vessels appeared. When they were removed, a vessel in the shape of a lion's head (or of a lioness or lion-cub) was found on the floor below, simpering a welcome to its belated rescuers. In full face, pensive; in half-profile, chubby and affable as on the day of its creation. *Plate* 16*d* *Plate* 17*a* *Plate* 17*b*

(*iii*) *The north room.* 'Still more dramatic', in the words of Marinatos, 'was the excavation of the adjoining magazine 3 to the north, where big jars, medium-sized vases, little pots and stone vessels and implements were literally heaped together'. 'The most beautiful pots, both local and imported, were found in this room'. One of them concealed a surprise. At the bottom of the jar, under the filling of pumice, a small figurine was found lying on a bed of dark organic matter, perhaps flour. She was surely divine; but she was neither beautiful nor expensive. She was made of unbaked clay. She had a long neck and not much other shape; she was indeed 'flat as a board'. She was taken to the Museum, and there her brief resurrection ended; she vanished, perhaps simply dissolved. *Plate* 17*c* *Plate* 17*d*

It is obvious that this tripartite store-room, whose floor-space measures about 480 square feet, was congested with equipment and stores. The owner of this house kept an uncommonly large and well-provisioned larder, and liked to have decorative things about him.

Opposite the store-room on its west side, but on an upper floor, is a room which may make an important addition to our knowledge of the inhabitants. It appears to be a room reserved for divine worship. Some of its contents were found *in situ*, others had fallen through the collapsed floor into the middle store-room:

Plate 18*a*: A circular table with saucer-like depressions for ritual offerings. The surface is painted. *Plate* 18*a*

Plate 18*b*: A vessel for libation; nippled jug, with painting of barley-stalks. *Plate* 18*b*

Plate 18*c*: A libation-jug, decorated with continuous spirals and with branches on the shoulder. Imported from Crete. *Plate* 18*c*

Plate 18*d*: A conical rhyton, found close to the vetch-jug and the swallow bath-tub (pp. 30f. above). *Plate* 18*d*

These are not vessels for the table or the kitchen or the larder; they are for the service of the gods. And the reservation of a room for domestic worship may throw some light on

III SANTORINI: THE BURIED TOWN

the relation between the Santorini settlement and Crete. The wall-paintings and import of Cretan pottery prove commercial and cultural contact with Crete; but they are far from proving that the Santorini residents were Cretans. Now the domestic cult-room is (at least in this period) characteristic of Crete, not of Mycenaean Greece; and it seems a probable inference that the occupants of this house were Cretans, worshipping Cretan gods with the Cretan ritual-vessels found in and near this room. It will be natural to suppose that the island was controlled by these Cretan settlers living so prosperously in their comfortable and well-equipped mansions; but we do not know (and it is doubtful if we shall ever know) whether they were politically independent of their Cretan motherland.

Excavation could now proceed westward only by tunnelling. There are obvious disadvantages in this procedure, but the objections to the normal method, tersely stated by Marinatos, are at present unanswerable; it 'would be a very costly process. It would also alter for the worse the aspect of the landscape, deprive the inhabitants of Acrotiri of the use of their meagre fields, and require very large expenditure to cover the cost of the expropriations'.

Plate 19 The Western Tunnel was about 50 m. long in 1969. Plate 19 gives an impression of the tunnel, with a window and adjacent doorway. There is much pottery on the floor of the tunnel. At one point a foot of drainage-pipe sticks out of the wall into the passage.

I have offered a very slight sketch of a complex site, and a very small selection of illustrations of its contents. This is one of the most interesting and potentially rewarding excavations of our time. Whatever the future may reveal (and many years of difficult work lie ahead), it is already plain that a prosperous settlement in this area, contemporary with Late Minoan I a in Crete, was totally destroyed, first by earthquake, then soon afterwards by a huge downpour of pumice. The evidence of the relics proves that the destruction in Santorini preceded the destruction in Crete by at least a couple of decades. It throws no other direct light on the relation of the volcano's activity to the desolation of Crete; and to that relation I now turn.

[*Addendum* (September 1970). Great progress has been made at Acrotiri in the present season. The above account needs at least the following modifications:

1. P. 30 *Wall-paintings*: the stock of these is now immensely increased. Some of the frescoes are of great interest and originality; one of them is of exceptional beauty.

2. P. 30 *Size*: it is now known that Bronos 1A and 2 ('B' and 'D' in fig. 19, p. 29) are parts of a single mansion about 80 metres long and relatively narrow; it is more than twice as long as the longest mansion at Tylissos. There is now evidence also of three storeys above ground.

3. P. 30 *The contents* (and p. 32, last paragraph): a number of large and handsome bronze utensils have been found.

4. P. 32 The evidence for earthquake is now at one point (behind the threshold in Bronos 1A) most impressively re-inforced.]

IV   Crete: How the End Came

The problem confronting the historian may be briefly defined thus: In the period called 'Late Minoan I b', probably not far from 1450 B.C., all the known sites in eastern and central Crete, excepting Knossos, were destroyed. The list of casualties is impressive: the palaces of Phaestos, Mallia, and Zakro; the towns of Palaekastro, Gournia, Pseira, and Mochlos; great mansions at Nirou Khani, Amnisos, Tylissos, and Sklavókampo. I might have added Apodhoulou and Mitropolis and the collapsed cave at Arkalokhori.[1] I have omitted Vathypetro because the date of its destruction is probably a little earlier.[2] Some of the destroyed places were abandoned for ever; some were re-occupied, but not until later and then on a much smaller scale than before.

The general destruction of a civilization and the abandonment of its site, especially at a time of great material prosperity and high achievement in arts and crafts, arouses a natural curiosity and calls for a particular explanation. If human agency is ruled out, as I believe it should be, the theory proposed by Professor Marinatos may well appear the most probable alternative.

On the one hand we observe in Crete a pattern of general destruction; on the other we observe at Santorini a huge volcano-crater and an enormous deposit of pumice and ash attesting a volcanic eruption probably unsurpassed from that day to this. How far is it possible to confirm the suggestion that the volcanic eruption and the destruction of Crete are related as cause and effect? We have seen good reason to believe, in general, that volcanic activity on so huge a scale must have inflicted damage on land so close to the volcanic centre; but we need something more explicit. Is there any objective evidence that the volcano of Santorini not merely could have been or should have been, but actually was, responsible for the desolation of Crete in Late Minoan I b?

There are two articles of evidence which are not in dispute.

First, there is no doubt that volcanic ash was deposited on Crete in the Late Minoan period. In 1965 two members of the Lamont Geological Observatory at Columbia University, D. Ninkovich and B. Heezen, published a paper entitled 'The Santorini Tephra'.[3] A Swedish expedition (the *Albatross*) had already in 1947-8 extracted cores from the eastern Mediterranean sea-bed containing two separate layers of volcanic ash and had already related the upper layer to the Santorini ash-mantle. Additional cores containing volcanic ash were extracted by the *Vema* in 1956 and 1958. The evidence from both sources was studied by Ninkovich and Heezen, whose results, so far as they are relevant to my present purpose, are briefly summarized as follows.

Fourteen cores containing layers of volcanic ash were extracted by the *Vema*, seven by the *Albatross*. Of these twenty-one cores, sixteen contain one layer of ash and five contain two layers. The upper (or younger) layer is distinguishable from the lower (or older) layer by the refractive index of the glass of which the ash is largely composed and by examination of fauna and other sediments with which the ash is associated. It is therefore possible, where only one ash-layer is present in a core, to determine whether it belongs to the younger or the older class. The younger layer is certainly present in five cores; and the

---

[1]Apodhoulou: *AA* 1934, 248; 1935, 246. Mitropolis (a little south of Agii Dheka on the edge of the Mesara): Levi 251. Arkalokhori: Marinatos, *AA* 1934, 252; 1935, 244; Marinatos[1] 20.

[2]Vathypetro: Marinatos, *PAE* 1952, 592-610; Marinatos[1] 66, 68; Graham 72.

[3]See Bibliography.

IV CRETE: HOW THE END CAME

total has been increased by the results of a subsequent expedition reported to the Thera Congress by Dr Ryan. The dates of these ash-layers are roughly determined by the carbon-14 age of associated sediments. The older layer (now known to come from Ischia, not Santorini)[4] is *c.* 25,000 years old. Of the younger layer (which certainly comes from Santorini) no more can be demonstrated by this method than that it is less than *c.* 5,000 years old. And this conclusion is satisfactory enough. For the eruptions which left the present ash on Santorini must have left ash on the sea-bed; and if deposits of Santorini ash are found on the sea-bed which may be referred to those eruptions, common sense tells us that they not only may be but must be. There is no other submarine layer of Santorini ash in this period or anywhere near it, and there has been no other colossal eruption at Santorini since the one securely dated by buildings under the pumice to the Late Minoan period.

Attempts have been made to define the date more precisely by the carbon-14 age of material found under the pumice on Santorini. One of the most promising specimens so far is the trunk of a small (and therefore presumably young) olive-tree found upright and well-preserved under the pumice at Phira.[5] Earlier dates for this specimen range from *c.* 1,600 to *c.* 1,400 B.C., with a strong preference for a date not far from 1,500. Later and more refined methods provide the date *c.* 1,800 B.C.[6]; but as the pumice undoubtedly fell in the first Late Minoan period, this date is (to use a mild term) paradoxical.

For us, at the moment, the most important fact about these cores from the sea-bed is their distribution:

Fig. 19

The diagram indicates that the ash-cloud was carried in a south-easterly direction from Santorini. The cores containing the upper layer come from an area south and east of the volcano. This layer was not identified in any of thirteen cores extracted from the perimeter of the area shown, but it would be premature to draw significant conclusions from that fact. The number of samples is small, and Dr Ryan's researches, while confirming the easterly

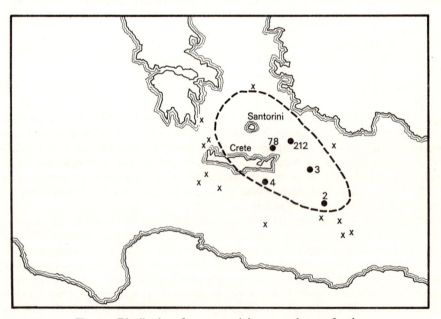

Fig. 19 Distribution of cores containing young layers of tephra
(numbers = thickness of layer in centimetres; × = absence of layer)

[4]Dr Ryan, report to the Thera Congress.   [5]Marinatos[2] 55 f., Luce 63 f.
[6]Professor Rainey, report to the Thera Congress.

IV CRETE: HOW THE END CAME

trend, have already extended the limits of the area. The south-easterly trend has been used as evidence that the great eruption occurred in summer, when north-westerly winds prevail in the Aegean, but the meteorological records displayed to the Thera Congress by Professor Carapiperis demonstrated that north-westerly winds are among the commonest in winter as well as in summer; from the mere fact that the wind was blowing from the north-west, you could not tell whether the month was July or January.

The point of cardinal importance is that the eastern half of Crete is straddled by the cores; they were found both north and south of the coast. It is therefore absolutely certain that volcanic ash was deposited on the eastern half of Crete; and we shall ask presently what the depth of the deposit may have been.

The second article of undisputed evidence is the discovery of human habitations immediately under the pumice-layer on Santorini; and there is now a large quantity of material attesting that the pumice destroyed the Santorini dwellings in the mature phase of Late Minoan I a, appreciably earlier than the destruction of Crete.

There is no other objective evidence of the effect of volcanic activity on Crete in this period except the following, of which the evidential value is questionable:

(i) A room full of pumice at Amnisos. No other part of the dwelling has been excavated. The pumice may have been carried by sea-floods from the Santorini volcano.[7]

(ii) Pumice was found widely scattered over the destruction-levels at Zakro. Other materials from Zakro, still awaiting analysis, were inspected by scientists at the Thera Congress. Their provisional opinion was that neither the pumice nor any other material from Zakro consists of airborne ejecta from Santorini; 'the specimens we saw at the Heraclion Museum', says Professor Heezen,[8] 'were made of limestone and brick. They were definitely not volcanic'.

This catalogue of physical evidence would be longer (but not very much) if my theme were not limited to the effect of the volcano on Crete but extended to include a wider survey. It would be necessary to consider especially:

(iii) evidence for the destruction of settlements closely related to Minoan culture in or about this period at Keos, at Cythera, and at Trianda in Rhodes;

(iv) the discovery of a layer of ash on the recent limestone on the island of Paros forty miles north of Santorini;[9]

(v) the discovery of pumice-layers very high up at the heads of ravines and valleys on the island of Anáphi fourteen miles east of Santorini;[10]

(vi) a pumice-layer five metres above sea-level on the coast of Palestine north of Jaffa.[11]

I return to the difficulty about the dating. It is certain that the Santorini settlements were destroyed by the great pumice-fall in Late Minoan I a; but Minoan Crete was destroyed in Late Minoan I b. At least a decade or two elapsed between the two catastrophes. The archaeological evidence requires two volcanic eruptions separated by an interval of this order of magnitude—one eruption depositing the great pumice-layer and burying the Santorini habitations, another of much greater violence at a later date depositing the huge layer of ash on Santorini and causing the desolation of Crete. This apparently necessary conclusion is in harmony with the findings of Reck and Georgalas, the leading authorities on the vulcanology of Santorini; it did not commend itself to a number of eminent vulcanologists who inspected a section of the quarries at Phira one afternoon in September 1969. These were of the opinion that the whole mantle, from the lowest pumice to the topmost ash, may represent and indeed probably does represent a

[7]Marinatos[4]. [8]*Saturday Review* 6 December 1969 p. 89.
[9]Sonder, *Zeitschr. Vulk.* viii (1924-5) 181 ff.
[10]Marinos & Melidhonis, *Gk. Geol. Soc.* iv (1959-61) 210 ff.
[11]Pfannenstiel, *Bull. de l'Inst. oceanogr.* 1192 (1960).

single paroxysmic eruption-phase. If this were so, the historian would have to accept the paradoxical conclusion that neither ash-fall nor sea-floods generated by the alleged colossal eruption had any significant effect on Crete, where almost all the sites are known to have flourished without serious interruption throughout Late Minoan I a into Late Minoan I b. This is not, I think, a credible conclusion. The archaeological evidence is clear and decisive. There must have been (as Professor Georgalas told the Thera Congress) a quite long interval between the deposition of the great pumice-layer and the deposition of the great ash-layer. We must at the same time admit that the behaviour of the Santorini volcano was very eccentric. Eruptions of this type and of this degree of violence occur as a rule in a single phase after a long period of quiescence. Tambora, Coseguina, and Bezymianny had been thought to be extinct; Cracatoa had not erupted for two hundred years;[12] Katmai had probably been dormant for centuries.[13] And none of these took more than a year to begin and end its final paroxysm.

Volcanic activity on Santorini might affect Crete in three ways: by deposit of ash; by sea-flooding; and (though not directly) by earthquake. It is immediately plain that neither ash-fall nor sea-flooding will explain the collapse of the monumental palace of Phaestos, five miles inland from the south coast and more than two hundred feet above sea-level; or of Tylissos (600 feet) or of Sklavókampo (higher still). Most of the other places could have been destroyed by sea-floods, but there is unmistakeable evidence that they were not. We have been collecting facts; and it is now time to recall and to emphasize a fact too little if at all appreciated—the fact that fire was a principal agent in the destruction of most of the Cretan sites in Late Minoan I b. There were devastating fires at Zakro, at Tylissos, at Sklavókampo, at Gournia, at Palaekastro, at Nirou Khani, at Phaestos and Hagia Triadha; there was burning at Mallia and Amnisos. Burning cannot be a consequence of sea-flooding under ancient conditions, though it may easily be under modern. If a wall of water seventy feet high broke at high speed over (say) Gournia, the village would be destroyed and everything inflammable would be rendered non-inflammable. If Gournia was destroyed by fire, it is very obvious that the fire preceded the flood—if there was a flood. Nor is there the remotest possibility that the fires were caused by the fall of hot ash or other ejecta from the volcano; the distance is much too great—eighty miles to Gournia, still more to Palaekastro and Zakro. There is only one readily acceptable alternative: the destruction of the large and solidly built palaces and mansions must have been caused by earthquake.

It is particularly to be stressed that the places which were destroyed by fire must have been already in ruins before the floods—if there were any floods—arrived on the shore of Crete. If anyone is inclined to doubt this, let him ponder the implications of the following extract from the excavation-report on Gournia:

> 'The conflagration which destroyed the town left proof of its strength in many parts of the excavation. Wooden posts and steps were entirely burned away, leaving deposits of charcoal and marks of smoke-grime; bricks were baked bright red. In a ground-floor room of the Palace lay a large tree-trunk which had supported an upper floor, completely charred through, but retaining its original shape; the Central Hall of the Palace was choked with such timbers. Limestone was calcined, steatite was reduced to crumbling fragments; in a doorway of the Palace lay a shapeless lump of bronze, once the trimmings of the door. Strangest of all was the effect on plaster ... The intense heat re-converted it into unslaked lime, and this, under the first rain, again formed plaster, encasing vases, or anything else on which it fell, in an airtight, almost petrified mass'.[14]

It is perfectly obvious that there could have been no such effects of fire in a village which had been already flooded and flattened by a gigantic sea-wave.

[12] *RS* 10.   [13] Wilcoxson 25.   [14] *Gournia* (see p. 5 n. 6) 21.

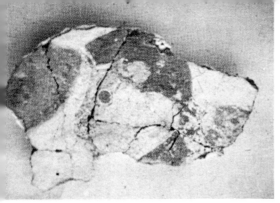

Plate 9a Acrotiri, monkey, wall-painting

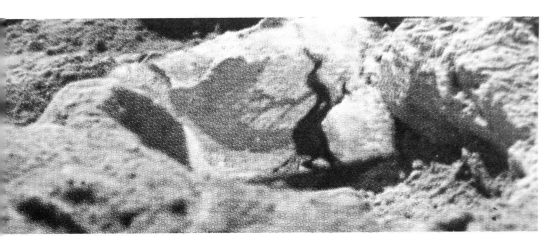

Plate 9b Acrotiri, flying bird, wall-painting

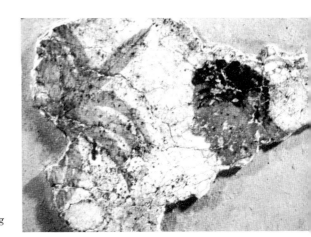

Plate 9c Acrotiri, man and palm tree, wall-painting

Plate 9d Acrotiri, a flagstoned floor

Plate 10a Acrotiri, basement with window at street level

Plate 10b Acrotiri, interior service-stair

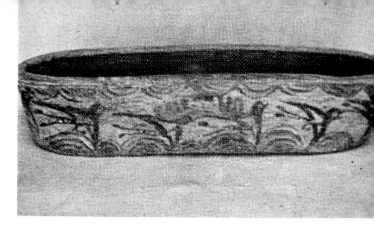

Plate 11b   Acrotiri, kymbe with swallows

Plate 11a   Acrotiri, decorated strainer

Plate 11c   Acrotiri, polychrome jug

Plate 11d   Acrotiri, kymbe with dolphins

Plate 12a Acrotiri, spherical jug

Plate 12b Acrotiri, spherical jug

Plate 12c Acrotiri, spherical jug

Plate 12d Acrotiri, goblets and a cup

IV CRETE: HOW THE END CAME

Destruction is one thing, abandonment another. If earthquake and fire destroyed the places, what caused them to be wholly abandoned? The answer must be given by the depth of the ash-deposit on Crete; what was it? Is there any means of inferring, from the thickness of a core from the sea-bed, what the depth of the ash was on adjacent land at the time of its falling? One of the *Albatross* cores, *c.* 35 km. south of eastern Crete, and one of Dr Ryan's, *c.* 20 km. south of central Crete, contain a layer 4 cm. thick; what was the depth on the nearest coast when the ash fell 3,500 years ago? A precise answer is not to be expected, but it would be useful if an answer could be given to the more limited question: is it certain, or at least very probable, that the depth on land will have been great enough to render that land uninhabitable for a decade or a generation?

The layman wonders whether ash which has lain so long with heavy sediments above it and a huge weight of water above that may not be much compressed, so that 4 cm. in a core might represent only a tiny fraction of the original thickness; but he will be told that the degree of compression is in fact very small. It is agreed, however, that the thickness on the sea-bed will be appreciably less than that of the deposit on adjacent land, because only a proportion of the ash which falls on a given area of sea-surface will finally settle below that area; and allowance must be made for the fact that the land-surface in question here is much closer to the volcano than the areas from which the cores were extracted.

In a case where comparison could be made by measurement, Dr Keller states[15] that the ratio was 5 on land to 1 on the sea-bed. We have therefore to accept the general likelihood that the original depth on the south coast of Crete was at least 20 cm., and it is to be expected that the depth was greater in the centre and still greater in the north of the areas affected.

What would be the effect on these areas of an ash-deposit of such depths? I refer to Professor Thorarinsson's evidence concerning the effect of ash-deposits in Iceland: 7 cm. of ash in its present compressed state on land has caused temporary abandonment of sites, and 15 cm. of ash in its present compressed state on land has caused permanent abandonment; the original depth being estimated as between two and three times the present depth.[16] It will therefore seem probable that the depth on the south coast of Crete caused temporary abandonment, and practically certain that the greater depths in the centre and north caused abandonment for at least a decade or two. I do not see how it is possible at present to be more precise; but even this limited answer is of value; it explains what nothing else has ever explained—why neither the Minoans nor anyone else made any attempt to re-occupy their devastated sites for an appreciable period of time. The cause of the fires which resulted in the destruction of the Minoan sites may remain somewhat enigmatic, but there is no longer any reasonable doubt about the cause of the abandonment.

And now I cannot refrain from expressing the opinion that the suggested depth of the deposit on Crete may be a great deal less than the truth. Smaller eruptions have left much deeper deposits at comparable distances in modern times. I have already noted that the rate of deposit from Cracatoa was three feet an hour at forty miles distance. The eruption of the Alaskan volcano Novarupta in 1912 was 'sufficient to bury deeply several thousand square miles of the surrounding region'[17]; at a distance of thirty-five miles from the cone the deposit was ten feet deep[18]; and at Kodiak, a hundred miles away, 'the weight of the ash which accumulated on roofs was sufficient to cause houses to collapse'.[19] According to Sir Stamford Raffles, the ash-deposit from Tambora in 1815 lay three feet deep in Java at a distance of three hundred miles from the volcano.[20] It is obviously probable that the depth in eastern Crete was to be measured rather in metres than in centimetres. What is most needed now is a much larger number of cores from the sea-bed; a hundred, taken

---

[15] At the Thera Congress.
[16] Report to the Thera Congress; *Acta Islandica* 2 (1958) 1-100; Luce 91 f.
[17] Cotton 194.   [18] Wilcoxson 27.   [19] Cotton 194.   [20] Wilcoxson 124 f.

IV CRETE: HOW THE END CAME

from all round the coast of Crete, might be enough for a reliable isopach-diagram. At present we cannot be sure which comes closer to the average—*Albatross* 192 with its 4 cm. or *Vema* 58 with its 78 cm.

If the very low estimate of 20 cm. is accepted, with greater depths in the centre and the north, it is still certain that the eastern half of Crete must have been uninhabitable for some time (except in the neighbourhood of Knossos). All livestock, and any humans who stayed, must have died of thirst or starvation, as fifty thousand died on the islands within reach of the Tambora ash-fall in 1815-6. Moreover in historical times the Santorini volcano has emitted vast quantities of sulphate and chloride during its major eruptions; if these affected Minoan Crete, the damage to the soil would be so much the greater.[21] And in the days following the ash-fall the deposits in fertile valleys and plains might become thicker, not thinner. Two thirds of Crete are mountainous. The mountains are the first to lose their deposit; winds and rains carry much of it down the slopes to lower ground. On the day after the eruption of Novarupta 'avalanches of ashes could be heard sliding on the neighbouring hills'[22] near Kodiak, a hundred miles from the volcano. The plains and valleys of central and eastern Crete will have remained sterile deserts of ash for some years.

How many years? Ten, or twenty, or fifty, or what? Suppose (for example) that the depth was a metre in the north, diminishing gradually to the south; how long a time elapsed before the ash ceased (more or less) to be visible on the surface; and should we expect to find traces of it today?

In general, the process of elimination varies according to a number of conditions, of which the most important (after the depth) are the climate and character of the land. The process will be slower on forested than on unforested land; slower on light than on heavy soil. In areas exposed to the violence of tropical rains the elimination of a metre of ash may be very rapid. The rains of a single season dispersed an ash-deposit one metre deep over a circle of twenty miles diameter after the eruption of Niuafoo in the Tonga Islands in 1886.[23] When Matupi and Vulcan erupted in 1937 the ash on Rabaul lay more than a metre deep;[24] it was not easy to find much trace of that deposit a few years later. The process will have been much slower in Crete: the soil is generally light; the island was thickly forested; and the rains are not to be compared with the tropical. Nevertheless the rains are heavy enough, and the winds strong and constant enough, to make good progress in the dispersal and elimination of a metre of ash; if the depth was indeed no greater than this, it may be doubted whether much of the deposit remained visible after (say) a couple of decades. The grains of wind-borne ash are minute and volatile; 'fifty miles from a volcano-vent, the average ash-flake is ten times smaller than a grain of sand'.[25]

Is it likely that any remnant of such a deposit would be detectable after 3500 years? I am not aware that any attempt has ever been made to identify volcanic ash in the soil of Crete, either in archaeological excavations or elsewhere; nor have I heard of the identification of an ash-layer in geological studies of the island. Analysis of soil-samples from excavations, and drilling on so promising a site as the plain of Lasithi, might help. But if (as I am told) it is likely that ash-particles in the soil will have become devitrified in so long a time, I wonder whether the ash, if any exists, can now be identified with certainty as volcanic. I should like to be refuted by experiment; meanwhile I remain sceptical of the likelihood of identifying, below the surface of the earth in Crete, volcanic ash from the layer deposited in the Minoan period.

I have concentrated so far on the ash-fall over Crete; justifiably, I think, because whatever else may have happened, the cores from the sea-bed assure us that this did happen. And it is the one and only effect of volcanic action which could have rendered a large part of Crete uninhabitable for some time. It remains to consider the other possible effects, notably sea-flooding and earthquakes.

[21]*Cf*. Ninkovich and Heezen 432f.   [22]Wilcoxson 27.   [23]Wilcoxson 151.
[24]Wilcoxson 153.   [25]Heezen, *Saturday Review loc. cit.* (p. 37, note 8).

IV CRETE: HOW THE END CAME

1 *Flood-waves*. I have already given a few facts and figures about the effect of these following the much smaller eruption at Cracatoa in 1883. I recall now that at one point about a mile inland the wave was still forty feet high; at another, a gunboat was picked up and stranded thirty feet above sea-level almost two miles inland[26] (it is said to be still there).[27] The fall of immense masses of ash in the sea around Santorini, and especially the final disintegration of the volcano, must have generated large sea-floods. But we must not assume that the main direction taken by the flood-waves was toward Crete. We must remember that North Watcher Island, eighty-two miles over the open sea north of Cracatoa, saw nothing of the huge sea-floods generated on 27 August—or nothing but a wave eight feet high on arrival.[28] The seismic activity which accompanied the eruption of Santorini in July 1926 created a huge flood-wave; and this took an easterly direction, standing eighty feet high on arrival at Amorgos, 32 km. distant to the north-east; westward, at Pholegandros, 43 km. distant, the wave was only half as high (33 ft.). There was no effect upon Crete, except a six-foot wave on its north-eastern coast.[29] If the flood-waves in Late Minoan I took an easterly track, we could easily account for the great altitude of the pumice-deposits on Anáphi, a few miles east of Santorini, and the thick belt of pumice on the coast of Palestine. The effect on Crete may have been relatively slight; and there is reason to believe that it was in fact very slight indeed.

The speed of such flood-waves increases according to the depth of the water over which they pass. The calculated speed for such a wave on arrival at the north coast of Crete from Santorini—assuming that this was the direction taken by the wave—is *c.* 200 m.p.h.;[30] about twenty minutes after leaving the volcano, the wave would have reached Crete at this speed. Calculations of the height of the wave on arrival vary so greatly—from 25 m. to 200 m.—that the layman is at a loss. But if the lowest estimate is accepted, a wall of water 75 feet high at 200 miles an hour would have left nothing standing at Pseira, Mochlos, Nirou Khani, Gournia, and Amnisos. The actual ruins do not at all suggest destruction by flood-waves of this degree of violence; and in fact it is certain that Gournia and Nirou Khani were destroyed by fire, not flood. It is no good saying that Gournia (for example) might have received the flood-wave after its destruction by fire; for it is perfectly obvious that if Gournia had been overrun by even a small flood, there would not have been any little heaps of charcoal or plaster left *in situ* for the excavators to find. Gournia is a test case. And it tells us in plain terms that there never was a big sea-flood on the north coast of Crete in Late Minoan I. Standing on a low elevation very close to the shore, it was exposed to the full force of a sea-flood moving south from Santorini. The flood cannot have passed over it before its destruction by fire, for there would have been nothing left to burn. And the flood cannot have passed over it after its destruction by fire, for the flood would have destroyed most of the evidence of the fire and many of the relics which were found *in situ* and intact. Gournia never was flooded, by big wave or small—at least not until the earth had had time to entomb the whole site, including rooms with walls still standing six feet high. The smallest flood would have disposed of those neat little heaps of charcoal, still in their proper places awaiting the excavator in 1901; to say nothing of that 'large tree-trunk, completely charred through, but retaining its original shape'.

2 *Earthquake*. If earthquake was the primary cause of destruction, it was not for the first time. About 1700 B.C. the great palaces of Knossos, Phaestos, and Mallia, to say nothing of lesser places, collapsed in a stupendous earthquake. And evidence is not wanting, though it falls short of proof, that earthquake was again the primary cause of destruction in Late Minoan I b. Doro Levi is confident that it was the cause at Phaestos; Sinclair Hood thinks it a likely cause of such damage as was done at Knossos at this time; it is the

[26] *RS* 93.
[27] Furneaux 109; he describes the *Berouw* as 'a vessel having a draft of six feet, carrying four guns, and having a complement of four Europeans and twenty-four natives'.
[28] *RS* 106.   [29] Tazieff 80.   [30] Ninkovich and Heezen 438.

only likely cause (sea-floods now being eliminated) for the collapse of the solid stone houses of Pseira. The state of the ruins and relics at Amnisos and Mallia and Zakro appears compatible with earthquake and hard to reconcile with any other cause. And earthquake is the likeliest cause of the widespread conflagrations.

That an earthquake of exceptional violence should precede an eruption of exceptional violence is in accord with experience. We know, as it happens, that the eruption which destroyed the Santorini settlements was preceded by an earthquake which reduced large buildings to a few courses of stone on the ground-floor. We know too that the great eruption of Santorini in 1650 was preceded for a year by earthquakes of exceptional violence; one of these, two weeks before the volcanic climax, is said to have affected every island in the Aegean.[31] The eruption of Santorini in 1926 was followed by an earthquake which destroyed fifty houses in Heraclion, damaged three hundred, and wrecked some of the neighbouring villages.[32] The eruption of Cracatoa in 1883 was preceded in 1880 by an exceptionally severe earthquake.[33] The great eruption of Bezymianny in Kamchatka in 1955-6 was preceded in November 1952 by an earthquake of one of the highest magnitudes ever recorded (8.25).[34] Other modern instances could be quoted; but we must not leap to the conclusion that the volcano causes the earthquake or vice-versa. Earthquakes are of two types, tectonic and volcanic. Tectonic earthquakes, which are caused by fractures, faults, slidings, and overthrusts in the earth's crust, 'make up more than ninety per cent of all the earthquakes that shake the world and a hundred per cent of the shocks of high magnitude'.[35] Although volcanic eruptions are always preceded, often accompanied, and sometimes followed by earthquakes,[36] yet the energy of a volcanic earthquake is seldom more than a very small fraction of that of a tectonic earthquake; the focus of its shocks is superficial, and damage is seldom done beyond the radius of a few kilometres. So I express no opinion about causal connexion; but there is no doubt whatever that violent tectonic earthquake has often preceded violent volcanic eruption in the same area. I am saying no more, but also no less, than that the evidence indicates that Minoan Crete was destroyed by a violent earthquake, followed after a short interval by one of the most violent volcanic eruptions of which we have any record.

There is, as it happens, a quite close parallel from modern Crete to what I suppose to have happened in ancient Crete. The only difference is in magnitude; the modern scale was large, the ancient was colossal. I refer to the exceptionally violent earthquake of 1856, which was followed ten years later by an exceptionally violent eruption at Santorini.

The earthquake of 12 October 1856 destroyed or damaged all but 18 of 3620 houses in Heraclion; and we note with interest that the 'overthrow was followed by a destructive fire in the bazaar'. Buildings which survived many previous shocks succumbed to this one; huge blocks from a church with walls of stone six feet thick resting on thicker foundations were thrown to a distance of two hundred yards. In the near-by village of Voutes 'no walls remained standing above a metre in height'. The shock passed along the north coast of Crete to the extreme east, then by way of the distant islands of Kasos and Karpathos to Rhodes, where great damage was done to the castle, towers, mosques, and houses; 'some minarets and houses fell in Cairo and Alexandria'.[37]

There is therefore nothing unprecedented in the hypothesis of a devastating earthquake in Crete accompanied by conflagrations and followed quite soon by an exceptionally violent eruption of the Santorini volcano. What happened in 1856-1866 may have happened in Minoan Crete; and the evidence strongly suggests that it did happen. You may object that in 1856 it was the district of Knossos which suffered most severely, whereas in the Minoan catastrophe that district suffered least; but the effect on Knossos depends on the depth and location of the seismic epicentre: 'An earthquake of intermediate focal

---

[31]Fouqué 12 f.   [32]Evans, *PM* ii 316 ff.   [33]*RS* 11.
[34]Tazieff 115.   [35]Tazieff 186.   [36]*Ibid.*; *cf.* Rittmann 42, on Coseguina.
[37]Evans, *PM* ii 315 ff., from which the quotations are taken.

Plate 13a Acrotiri, pot with pierced base

Plate 13b Acrotiri, jug with pendent sprays

Plate 13c Acrotiri, jug with reed-like plants

Plate 13d Acrotiri, sherds with 'Linear A' script

Plate 14a Acrotiri, doorway in wall affected by earthquake

Plate 14b Acrotiri, collapsed rubble wall

Plate 14c Acrotiri, displaced wall-blocks

Plate 14d Acrotiri, collapsed building

Plate 15a Acrotiri, window used as entrance

Plate 15b Acrotiri, blocked staircase

Plate 15c Acrotiri, 'Street of the Telchines'

Plate 15d Acrotiri, 'Street of the Telchines', cleared

Plate 16a Acrotiri, room occupied by 'squatters'

Plate 16b Acrotiri, a row of jars

Plate 16c Acrotiri, jars cracked by the heat

Plate 16d Acrotiri, broken vessels

Plate 17a Acrotiri, lion's head vessel, *in situ*

Plate 17b Acrotiri, lion's head vessel

Plate 17c Acrotiri, large decorated container

Plate 17d Acrotiri, small figurine in bottom of container

Plate 18a   Acrotiri, circular table with depressions

Plate 18b   Acrotiri, nippled jug

Plate 18d   Acrotiri, conical rhyton

Plate 18c   Acrotiri, libation jug

Plate 19 Acrotiri, window and door in Western Tunnel

Plate 20 Cloud from the cone of Bezymianny, 1956

IV CRETE: HOW THE END CAME

depth centred north near the central coast of Crete could account for the survival of Knossos in the epicentral halo of minor intensity'.[38]

If this explanation is correct in principle, the interval between earthquake and eruption must have been very short in the Minoan period; not ten years as in the nineteenth century, nor even ten months. Otherwise we should not be able to account for the fact that there was no attempt to re-build homes or even to recover objects of value from the floors.

It has been said that 'earthquakes . . . in ancient times are not liable to cause fires'; that 'these are the result of gas and electricity'.[39] No doubt conflagrations are more easily caused by earthquake in modern times, but it is not true that they were not so caused in ancient times. Sir Arthur Evans observed that 'at Candia and elsewhere, the ruin that an earthquake has brought has been followed at times by a wide conflagration';[40] there was no gas or electricity in most of the places he was thinking of. And ancient Cretan buildings were specially vulnerable to fire: palaces and houses included much inflammable material both in their construction and in their stores, and it is likely that their roofs (which were not tiled) were particularly vulnerable.

I am confident that the ash-deposit was the cause of the abandonment of the Cretan sites, but I should add that I have lately begun to consider with increasing sympathy a quite different explanation of their physical destruction. The final eruption of Cracatoa on 27 August 1883, and especially the colossal explosion at 10.02 on that day, cracked walls and overturned lamps at Batavia ninety-four miles away and at Buitenzorg a hundred miles away. No house collapsed; but we have to reckon with a very much bigger shock-wave from Santorini—if the final explosions were concentrated within a few hours as at Cracatoa. I wonder whether we need look further for the primary cause of the collapse of the buildings in Crete. 'If walls were cracked by aerial vibrations up to 160 km. from Cracatoa', says Luce, 'the mud-brick upper storeys of Cretan palaces and mansions could have suffered very severely from the same cause';[41] not merely could have, I should say, but must have. The question is rather whether buildings of the magnitude of Phaestos, Mallia, and Zakro could have been demolished by shock-waves from an eruption or series of eruptions very much greater than Cracatoa's. I do not know how to estimate the probability of this explanation. It would give a simple and sufficient account of everything, including the conflagrations; for the ash-cloud must have darkened the land for days before the final paroxysm, and lamps will have been burning by day as well as by night in Minoan Crete as in modern Java.

There is one other phenomenon which may be relevant to the present inquiry[42]—the movement of Cretans from the eastern to the western half of the island. The eastern half of Crete was much more populous than the western half in Minoan times, perhaps because the west was more densely forested and communications were more difficult except along the north coast. Recent explorations have shown that sites of the Middle Minoan period and earlier were commoner in western Crete than we had supposed,[43] so we must speak with caution; but it appears still probable that there was, as Pendlebury said, 'a particularly noteworthy . . . extension in the west'[44] at a time which may be relevant. This extension may have begun, or been accelerated, in the fifteenth century; and the ash-deposit on the eastern half of Crete is the only sufficient cause which has ever been advanced to explain why half the island—far the more populous and prosperous hitherto—was more or less abandoned while the other half became more densely populated. Neither ravages of earthquake nor military conquest will account for this particular phenomenon.

---

[38]Professor Galanopoulos, report to the Thera Congress. [39]Pendlebury 228.
[40]Evans, *PM* ii 320. [41]Luce 83. [42]*Cf.* Luce 93.
[43]Hood, *BSA* lx (1965) 99, lxii (1967) 47; Hood & Warren, *BSA* lxi (1966), 163; *cf.* Boardman, *On the Knossos Tablets* 87 n. 3.
[44]Pendlebury 237; *cf.* Hood, *BSA* lx (1965) 108.

IV CRETE: HOW THE END CAME

In summary, I take the following points to be proved beyond reasonable doubt:—

1. On the evidence of the ash-layer in the cores from the sea-bed: that central and eastern Crete were covered in volcanic ash to a depth too great for life to continue.

2. On the evidence from Gournia especially but also from other places: that the direction of the sea-floods generated by the great eruption of Santorini was not southward; the north coast of Crete was not flooded in this period.

3. On the evidence of the excavations in Crete: that most if not all the Cretan sites were destroyed by fire.

4. On the evidence of the artefacts in the destruction-levels in Crete and Santorini: that at least a couple of decades intervened between the pumice-fall which destroyed the Santorini settlements and the ash-fall which rendered the eastern half of Crete temporarily uninhabitable.

The most important matter remaining hypothetical is the cause of the fires which destroyed the Cretan sites. The most obvious explanation is earthquake; and I have given evidence that this is an explanation in accord with experience. A very attractive alternative, if it is tenable, is demolition by shock-waves.

Plate 20   I conclude with an illustration of the kind of cloud that buried in ash one of the most genial and artistically original civilizations in European history. It was photographed and measured in Kamchatka in 1956. It issues from the cone of Bezymianny. It is probably much smaller than the clouds which deposited the huge ash-layer on Santorini 3,500 years ago; but still it measures forty miles from the bottom to the top.

So much for the desolation of Minoan Crete.[45]

[45] I have said nothing about the Linear B tablets, because I find no relevant evidence in them. The only places whose identification in the eastern half of Crete seems to me certain are (apart from Knossos) Amnisos, Tylissos, Lyktos, and Phaestos. The mention of these places *c.* 1380 B.C. is entirely consistent with their destruction *c.* 1450 B.C.; no doubt they had all been re-occupied in the interval (Tylissos and Phaestos certainly had been).

Bibliography

List of works generally cited in notes by name of author only:

Banti, L.	*Il Palazzo Minoico de Festós* ii (1951).
Bullard F. M.	*Volcanoes in history, in theory, in eruption* (Nelson, Edinburgh 1962).
Cotton, C. A.	*Volcanoes as landscape-forms* (Christchurch, New Zealand, 2nd ed. 1952).
Desborough, V. R. d'A.	*The last Mycenaeans and their successors* (Oxford 1964).
Evans, Sir Arthur	PM = *The Palace of Minos* (Macmillan 1921-36).
Fouqué, F.	*Santorin et ses éruptions* (Paris 1879).
Furneaux, R.	*Krakatoa* (Secker & Warburg, London 1965).
Graham, J. W.	*The Palaces of Crete* (Princeton University Press 1962).
Hiller von Gaertringen, F.	*Die Insel Thera im Altertum und Gegenwart* (Berlin 1899).
Hood, M. F. S.	Hood[1] = *The Home of the Heroes* (Thames & Hudson 1967).
	Hood[2] = *Kadmos* iv (1965) 16 ff.
Hutchinson, R. W.	*Prehistoric Crete* (Pelican 1962).
Knidlberger, L.	*Santorin: Insel zwischen Traum und Tag* (Schloendorn Verlags-G.m.b.H., München 1965)
Lacy, A. D.	*Greek Pottery in the Bronze Age* (Methuen 1967).
Levi, D.	*Bollettino d' Arte* liv (1959) 251 ff.
Luce, J. V.	*The end of Atlantis* (Thames & Hudson 1969).
Marinatos, S.	Marinatos[1] = *Crete and Mycenae*, translated by J. Boardman (Thames & Hudson 1960).
	Marinatos[2] = *Excavations at Thera: first preliminary report* (1967 season) (Athens 1968).
	Marinatos[3] = *Excavations at Thera: second preliminary report* (1968 season) (Athens 1969).
	Marinatos[4] = *Antiquity* xiii (1939) 425-439.
Ninkovich, D. and Heezen, B.C.	'The Santorini Tephra'. *Submarine Geology and Physics: Proceedings of the seventeenth Symposium of the Colston Research Society* (London 1965).
Pendlebury, J. D. S.	*The Archaeology of Crete* (Methuen 1939).
Platon, N.	Platon[1] = *Crete* (F. Muller, London 1966).
	Platon[2] = *Ancient Crete*, by S. Alexiou, N. Platon, and H. Guanella (Thames & Hudson 1967).
Reck, H.	*Der Werdegang eines Insel-Vulkans und sein Ausbruch 1925-8* (De Gruyter, Berlin 1936).
Rittmann, A.	*Volcanoes and their activity*, translated by E. A. Vincent (London 1962).
RS = Royal Society	*The eruption of Cracatoa and subsequent phenomena: Royal Society Report*, edited by G. J. Symons (London 1888).
Tazieff, H.	*When the earth trembles* (Hart-Davis, London 1964).
Vermeule, E.	GBA = *Greece in the Bronze Age* (University of Chicago Press 1964).
Wilcoxson, K.	*Volcanoes* (London 1967).